The Art of Manifestation Astro-Moon Journal 2022

from the I Choose Love Series.
The Pathway of the Spiritual Warrior.

The Art of Manifestation

Astro-Moon Journal 2022

This Journal Belongs to

……………………………………………

The Art of Manifestation Astro-Moon Journal 2022
From the I Choose Love Series
The Pathway of the Spiritual Warrior

The Art of Manifestation Astro-Moon Journal
First Published 2019 A-Z of Emotional Health Ltd.

Published by the A-Z of Emotional Health Ltd.

The Art of Manifestation
Astro-Moon Journal

Welcome to 2022

Contents

My dear friends, in preparation for the publishing of this journal and its companion, The Art of Manifestation Astro-Moon Diary, I have been immersing myself in the astro-dynamics of 2022. Over the last year as I have delved deeply into my own process of manifestation, building a deepening connection with the Lunar cycles, my own depth of learning has been massively expanded. And so, this journal contains a whole new layer of learning that tunes into the tribal wisdom of the 13 Lunar phases of the year, with an emphasis on how to work with the energy of the New and Full Moons.

We are in the throes of an intense period of humanities evolution; indeed, I suspect that at a level of Soul, many of us have come here specifically at this time to play our part in our collective emergence into a new age. And yet, amidst the uncertainty and the challenges of the current happenings much opportunity for powerful and positive change is emerging. Old paradigms are crumbling, outworn attitudes, beliefs and behaviors are being called into question, and we are seeing a rising of passion and feeling that calls for equality, with new ways of thinking, doing, and being, that embrace respect, care, and regard. At this time of pivotal transition and rebirth, our circumstances are insisting on change and the Universe is demanding that we grow.

Thank you for using this journal and for choosing books like this to support your pathway. In the coming year of 2022, I send to you my love, my regard, and my deepest respect for the part that you are each personally playing in the emergence of this new dawn.

The Art of Manifestation

The art of manifestation involves not only imagining and dreaming of the kind of life that we wish to have, we must also take actions that enable our dreams to find form. Our state of mind, our attitudes and perceptions, and the way that we feel, our emotions, all have an impact on our ability to fully immerse ourselves in this creative process.

It seems to me that manifestation has its own cyclical and natural pattern of evolution.

- We listen to our desires, and we allow ourselves to dream.
- We imagine possibilities and we honor their potential.
- We evaluate and decide what steps we must take to initiate these possibilities into form.
- Remaining open to ongoing evaluation, we commit to a pathway forward.
- We persevere in our doing, trusting that any diversions and interruptions are sent to us to bring greater meaning, clarity, and direction.
- When needed, whether in our external actions or deep within our own psyche, we identify any ongoing work that we need to do to keep the energy flowing.
- We continue our ongoing pathway of evolution and co-creativity, and we trust that we will always be shown the next steps.
- Listening to the wisdom and guidance of the universe, when needed we course correct.
- Trusting that the universe knows of our fullest potential and holds a higher vision for us that is greater than we ourselves could possibly imagine, we understand that we will be given what we need, although not always necessarily what we want.
- Our pathway emerges and our dreams begin to take form.

How to Use this Journal

This journal can be used independently in its own right or used alongside the Art of Manifestation Diary. Both will assist you in understanding how best to align with and use, the incoming lunar and astro-energy to support your process of conscious manifestation.

The Journal is divided into thirteen sections each aligning with a Lunar phase, listing key astrological dates and Earth festivals, with information about the traditional Tribal and Celtic meanings of each Moon time and details of the astro-dynamics for each New and Full Moon. Alongside a selection of lined and clear pages for journaling there is also dedicated space to write your New Moon Wishes and Intentions and your Full Moon revelations and insights.

The journal also draws on the natural properties of a particular stone or crystal that aligns with the Lunar energy, with information about how these natural healers of the Earth can aid and support us, particularly during times of accelerated growth and transition.

In this journal you will find a section at the beginning with a list of the thirteen Tribal and Celtic phases of the Moon, information about manifesting with the Full and New Moons plus a description of the way that the lunar energy is affected and channeled as the Moon travels through each sign of the zodiac and the Void of Course 'space in-between'. I have also included sections about Solar and Lunar Eclipses and the influences of the various planets in retrograde and listed the dates that these events occur for this year.

To complete our understanding of how best to attune ourselves with the rhythms and cycles of the natural world, I have also shared some thoughts about the way in which we can navigate the shifts in energy that take place at the Earth festivals that mark the turning of the seasons, so we can fully appreciate and understand the relevance of these pivotal moments of natural transition in the context of our manifestations.

Working with the Tribal and Celtic Moons

Alongside my counselling practice of many years, fueled by the need to meet the challenges of my own life and also my desire to help others to overcome personal difficulties and live thriving fulfilled lives, I have been passionately learning about Moon phases and astro-energy and the natural lore's and wisdom held sacred by ancient traditions for a good while now.

When I began to look at the Native American understandings of the Lunar phases alongside Celtic Tree Lore I was blown away by the similarities of understanding connected to each phase of the Moon. What was even more amazing was that the more I read and linked in with the monthly teachings for each cycle, I realized that the circumstances of my own personal world, and those of others who I was working with, whilst unique and individual to us each, were a perfect reflection of the lessons presented in the tribal wisdom.

Having created the Art of Manifestation Astro-Moon diary to help build a deeply personal relationship with the cycles and phases of the Moon, with the empowerment that this brings to our lives, I decided to approach the Art of Manifestation Journal through the sharing of my own learning and experiences that have come from working with the thirteen Moon phases of Tribal understanding.

I am deeply indebted to the extraordinary work of Jamie Sams, whose gifted storytelling and profound wisdom opened up a whole new layer of growth and learning that for me has been lifechanging.

I also wish to honor the work of Jan Spiller whose insightful work enabled me to really understand how to work with the empowerment of the New and Full Moons.

The Thirteen Tribal and Celtic Moons 2022

- The First Moon Phase of 2022
  - Talks With Relations - Wolf Moon – Old Moon – Cold Moon - Birch Moon
- The Second Moon Phase of 2022
  - Wisdom Keeper - Snow moon – Hunger Moon – Bone Moon - Rowan Moon
- The Third Moon Phase of 2022
  - Weighs the Truth – Worm Moon – Sap Moon – Wind Moon - Ash Moon
- The Fourth Moon Phase of 2022
  - Looks Far Woman – Pink Moon – Planters Moon – Alder Moon
- The Fifth Moon Phase of 2022
  - Listening Woman – Flower Moon – Budding Moon – Willow Moon
- The Sixth Moon Phase of 2022
  - Storyteller – Strawberry Moon – Rose Moon – Hawthorn Moon
- The Seventh Moon Phase of 2022
  - Loves All Things – Buck Moon – Thunder Moon – Oak Moon
- The Eighth Moon Phase of 2022
  - She Who Heals – Sturgeon Moon – Green Corn Moon – Holly Moon
- The Ninth Moon Phase of 2022
  - Setting Sun Woman – Harvest Moon – Corn Moon – Hazel Moon
- The Tenth Moon Phase of 2022
  - Weaves the Web – Hunters Moon – Moon of Falling Leaves – Vine Moon
- The Eleventh Moon Phase of 2022
  - Walks Tall Woman – Beaver Moon – Frost Moon – Ivy Moon
- The Twelfth Moon Phase of 2022
  - Gives Praise – Cold Moon – Long Nights Moon – Reed Moon
- The Thirteenth Moon Phase of 2022
  - Becomes Her Vision – Elder Moon

The New and Full Moon

The New Moon.

Every New Moon marks the beginning of a new phase of tribal wisdom underpinning our process of evolution with the learning of each Lunar phase building upon the last.

New Moons are traditionally associated with the setting of wishes and intentions and so the energy at this time naturally invites us to meditate into a space of possibility. If you are a daily meditator, you may already find that for the two days before and the two days after the New Moon, your mind may be inclined to wander during your meditations. If this is the case you may find it helpful to have a pen and paper close by or use the journaling pages in this diary to make a note of any ideas that come to you during your meditation practice including any actions needed to move your ideas forwards.

Whilst frequently spoken of together, New Moon wishes, and New Moon intentions are actually different. A wish is embodied by the energy of the feminine and calls from the heart, inviting us to enter an internal creative space, and from within this dreamtime, formulate a clarity of desire. Whereas an intention is embodied by the masculine and asks us to formulate clear decisions that create pathways of action in the external world to move our dreams and desires into form.

Whatever your preferred way of finding stillness, calm your mind, and enter your own dreamtime. Let your mind wander into the depths of the New Moon energy and give yourself permission to dream big! Then take time to meditate further on your wishes before formulating your intended courses of action.

To align with the New Moon energy at its most powerful, be sure to write your wishes and intentions down during the 8 hours following the exact time of the New Moon in your location.

The Full Moon.

The Full Moon occurs when the Sun and the Moon sit directly opposite one another. The Moon has gathered light and energy from the Sun and shines at her brightest, illuminating all that needs to be seen. Use this time each month to meditate and request illumination and guidance to support your manifestations.

The full brightness of this powerful and highly charged energy brings a space of authenticity where all is revealed and illuminated, and so the Full Moon is often a time when we experience heightened and intense emotions.

Be kind to yourself and others. Notice and listen, particularly to any situations that are not okay. Things that are usually tolerated or brushed under the carpet will surface and request your attention. So, if you find yourself experiencing any challenging emotions please take them seriously. The energy of this phase of the Moon brings a wonderful opportunity to notice, to listen, to reflect, and then to release and let go, clearing the way to move forwards.

In the process of manifestation, if we find ourselves unable to move forwards or feel stuck in some way, it is often some aspect of our past that is still lingering, blocking us from believing in ourselves or believing in others or finding trust in the possibility of a different future. Anyone who has ever experienced trauma or abuse will tell you that whilst the physical scars will heal, it is the emotional ones that remain.

The Full Moon illuminates our emotions highlighting exactly what is working for us... as well as anything that is not!

Learn to differentiate between emotions that connect to past experiences, as opposed to emotions that are part of your immediate response system helping you to navigate your life in the here and now. There is a difference! Our emotions contain and generate energy. Understanding this difference between past and present emotional influences allows you to identify anything that you need to release from the past, empowering you to channel any highly charged emotional energy into positive action.

If you find yourself struggling with challenging emotional states, you may find 'Mindfulness Meets Emotional Awareness - 7 steps to learn the language of your emotions' a useful read. This book explains exactly how and why our most challenging emotions serve us and will teach you how to transform and channel any highly charged emotions into actions that support your pathway rather than hinder it.

If you work with healing stones and crystals, be sure to place them outside overnight to revitalize and recharge their energy for the coming month. You may also want to place some rainwater or spring water in a bowl and leave it out overnight to absorb the energy of the Full Moon. Do NOT use a plastic bowl! Use glass or earthenware or any container whose fundamental ingredients come from a natural source. Collect the water afterwards and store it in a jar for your ceremonies throughout the year.

The Moon in the Zodiac Signs

Moon in Aries.

At this emotionally powerful time, use the energy to be assertive and to initiate your ideas. Say how it is and take action.

Moon in Taurus.

Grounded, sensual, and earthy, use this energy to attune yourself with the natural rhythms of nature. A great time for walking meditations.

Moon in Gemini.

A time of communication, reaching out and connecting with others, use this energy for networking and socializing.

Moon in Cancer.

A wonderful time to be at home, share food and be in the company of family and close friends. Use this energy to nourish your soul, spending time with those you love.

Moon in Leo.

Sing, laugh, express yourself and find your voice. Use this energy to feel alive and embrace the joy of self-discovery and self-expression. We are never too old to play!

Moon in Virgo.

This energy supports us in attending to any work that requires dedication, structure, order and precision. Approach your tasks with willingness and a desire to serve.

Moon in Libra.

The energy of this Moon calls us to seek harmony and to find balance. This is a time to share and to discover ourselves through our relationships and the company of others.

Moon in Scorpio.

A time to journey inwards, this energy connects us to the depths of our unconscious and can bring deep emotions to the surface. Be sure to listen to yourself and take your yearnings seriously.

Moon in Sagittarius.

The energy of this Moon invites us to vision in an optimistic future, full of hope and possibility. A great time to expand our horizons and dream big!

Moon in Capricorn.

The energy of this Moon invites us to take pragmatic, practical actions to manifest our ideas into form. Get building and embrace the joy of doing.

Moon in Aquarius.

A time to collaborate, share ideas and work together. The energy of this Moon invites you to align your individual contribution with a higher vision of greater purpose that will also serve the collective Soul of humanity.

Moon in Pisces.

A time to dream and a time to heal. Open yourself to divine inspiration and allow yourself to be guided. The energy of this Moon brings illumination, fuelling imagination and creativity.

Void of Course Moon

As the Moon travels around the earth, it appears to us as if she passes through each of the 12 signs of the zodiac. Sometimes she will move directly from one sign to another, but at other times there is a space in between. This can last just a few minutes, or sometimes several hours. When the Moon is 'void of course', it means that she is transitioning through this space, in between two different signs.

As she travels through each sign of the Zodiac the powerful magnetism of her energy is channeled through the energetic resonance or personality of that sign. However, when she is void of course, there is a kind of energetic pause where her energy is no longer affected and guided by the influence of a particular sign.

I have noticed that this space of 'in betweenness' affects people in quite different and uniquely individual ways, depending on how they are feeling and what is taking place in the immediacy of their lives at any given time.

For some, this pause in the incoming energy of our beloved Moon, brings opportunity to be still and to release any goal driven targets, creating a natural channel for insights and illuminations to flow through. However, for others, particularly during periods of extreme change and transition, the void of course Moon can feel quite emotionally intense.

At some point in our lives, we will all experience challenging situations and circumstances, this is simply a part of our human journey. Indeed, it is often through periods of adversity that we find our greatest learning. But this doesn't mean it's easy! And at times of difficulty during our lives, we will inevitably experience some pretty intense emotions and when the Moon is void of course it can seem as though emotions are flooding in with no channel to direct or contain them.

In my experience it can pay dividends to notice how the void moon affects us and therefore to anticipate ahead of time how best to use this time. When life is running smoothly, we can actively anticipate using this time for periods of meditation, creating space and availability to receive insights and illumination. However, if life is not running smoothly, we can also actively anticipate using this time appropriately and we can become more consciously attentive in managing our diaries.

There will always be times when the incoming energy will support us in taking action and moving forwards, as well as times when it is more appropriate to hold back, to rest and to pause. Our awareness of the influences and impact of the incoming energy of the Moon and other planetary influences and the way that these affect us in a personal way enables us to become conscious in our decision-making and is therefore a valuable skill in the art of manifestation.

To access detailed daily information about the Moon positions including any void of course periods follow Jenny's Facebook page where she posts daily Lunar information.

https://www.facebook.com/azofemotionalhealth/

Solar and Lunar Eclipses

During eclipse season, the already intense energy of both the New and Full Moons are intensified. An eclipse in your sign, will always be a significant trigger point or turning point in your own personal process of evolution and can often herald random events that create sudden and unexpected changes.

On your personal journey of manifestation, understanding this heightened and intensified energy can be incredibly helpful in knowing, when to reflect and set your intentions, and when to take action to move something forwards, particularly if you intend to make or initiate significant changes in any aspect of your life.

Eclipses are also associated with our Karmic journey, creating an energetic rift that overrides our usual perception of and connection to time. The energy of the eclipses is said to open an energetic portal that assists us in connecting with our purpose and calling in this present lifetime.

Symbolized in the tarot pack by the cards of Death and the Tower, the energy of both the solar and lunar eclipses are associated with transformation, either internally or in the circumstances of our external lives, and often involves both endings and new beginnings.

When we learn to work with the influence of the eclipses, rather than trying to control events, we consciously make time to allow the energy of a greater universal consciousness to flow through us, bringing us the guidance that we need to support the evolution of our Soul within our human experience.

Solar Eclipse.

A solar eclipse is when the Moon sits in between the Sun and the Earth, with the Moon covering the Sun. This will always occur at a New Moon. The energy associated with this time is the same as a New Moon, but intensified, like a New Moon on steroids!

This is the perfect time to get still and to meditate into a space of personal dreamtime and allow your ideas to flow.

The energy of the solar eclipse can bring an extraordinary surge of creative possibilities, although these may not always arrive in the shape or form that we expect. If you are already involved in setting wishes and intentions, but then find that something happens to suddenly create a shift in your direction, trust that this unexpected change is important to your personal growth and evolution and connected to the calling of your soul.

In matters of manifestation, the universe will always have the upper hand and tends to bring us what we need... although not always what we want!

When we can allow ourselves to trust that even in moments of upheaval and disruption we are being gifted with an opportunity, we open ourselves to receive the fullest potential and the greatest learning to be found in every situation.

Lunar Eclipse.

A lunar eclipse is when the earth sits between the Moon and the Sun, and this will always occur at a Full Moon. Full Moons are associated with heightened emotions and during a lunar eclipse, emotions can run high, like a Full Moon on steroids!

If we think of the Moon as our Feminine Guardian who circles our planet, gathering the energy of the Sun and redistributing it to the Earth in various measures, at the time of a Lunar Eclipse, the energy of the Moon is like a fully charged battery, highly charged and ready to ignite change.

In the illumination of the Full Moon at her most powerful, all is revealed. Anything and everything that is running smoothly and working in service of a balanced and authentic life will be apparent to us, confirming that we are walking the right path. Likewise, anything and everything that is not working for us or no longer serves us, both internally and externally, will also be brought into the light, calling to be addressed, changed, and if necessary, released.

As long as something remains hidden or unconscious, we are helpless to address the issue and to take actions of resolution, however, when we identify a problem, the very fact that we can see the issue clearly creates an opportunity to seek solutions and find ways forward. On our personal journey of manifestation, the energy of a lunar eclipse increases our connections with any emotional residue from the past that may be clinging and coloring our perspectives inappropriately, creating an amazing opportunity for cleansing and release, clearing the way for resolution and healing. This is a powerful time to embrace forgiveness, of both ourselves and others.

Lunar eclipses are often associated with external changes that are a mirror or a reflection of our internal growth and learning. Whatever is taking place around you, if something in your life appears to be needing to change or to leave, let go gracefully and know that it is timely to the evolution of your soul.

If you are naturally a highly empathic person and particularly sensitive to the feelings of others, at the time of a lunar eclipse you may find yourself highly absorbent to the emotional states of the people around you. Be sure to cleanse and do a daily release ceremony to let go of anything that doesn't belong to you before meditating into your own space of illumination.

- **30th April – 20.42 GMT - New Moon Partial Solar Eclipse 10°35' Taurus**
- **16th May – 04.12 GMT - Full Moon Total Lunar Eclipse 25°16' Scorpio**
- **25th October – 11.01 GMT - New Moon Partial Solar Eclipse 02°07' Scorpio**
- **8th November – 11.00 GMT Full Moon Total Lunar Eclipse 15°59' Taurus**

The Planets in Retrograde 2022

The Inner Planets, Mercury, Venus, and Mars.

Mercury in Retrograde.

- **14th January 10° Aquarius – 4th February 24° Capricorn**
- **10th May 04° Gemini – 3rd June 26° Taurus**
- **10th September 08° Libra – 2nd October 24° Virgo**
- **29th December 24° Capricorn – 18th January 2023 08° Capricorn**

The energy of Mercury in retrograde is often associated with obstructions and delays, and in our target and goal orientated culture, we understandably tend to experience this period through a negative lens. Mercury retrograde periods seem to cause us no end of disruption, our plans go astray, we experience roadblocks and diversions, and there are often difficulties with our IT and communication systems.

However, if we step away from this viewpoint and consider that all aspects of planetary influences can support us and bring us valuable and necessary gifts, this shift in our perspective enables us to stand back and work with the incoming energy.

If there is a diversion, then the universe may be giving you a sign, perhaps you are meant to take an alternative route where you will discover something that was absolutely essential to your personal growth and evolution.

If something from your past raises its head during a Mercury retrograde period, then your attention is required. This is an invitation for you to acknowledge this issue and take time to embark on the necessary steps to lay it to rest.

There will always be times in our lives when the energy is with us to set targets and remain fixed on our course, to plough forwards and to push and to strive, however, given that the energy of Mercury represents our capacity to develop and integrate wisdom on our souls' journey within the human experience, when the Winged Messenger of the Gods temporarily stands still in the heavens and appears to travel backwards, this energy calls us back and asks us to slow down, to take our time and to be alert to any signals and signs that the universe is trying to show us.

Venus in Retrograde.

- **19th December 2021 26° Capricorn – 29th January 11° Capricorn**

Are you in balance? Do you allow yourself to receive as much as you give and vice versa? Are you actively involved in your own self-care? Do you pause to celebrate your achievements along the way, and do you give yourself an appropriate amount of time out to relax?

Self-care is not an act of selfishness; it is an act of consciousness.

When Venus moves into retrograde the energy of the feminine invites you to listen to your heart, to override the demands of a busy mind and be centered in your truest values, including and especially your own self-care.

Venus is in retrograde is a wonderful time to reflect and to realign and rebalance all areas of your life. This revitalizing influence of this phase will keep your energy clean and flowing and ensure that your energetic resonance is congruent with all that you wish to manifest into the world. As such, Venus in retrograde plays an essential role in our ability to manifest our truest desires.

During periods of transition, if you have ever found yourself questioning what your true calling might be, when Venus is in retrograde, ask for guidance and be open to receive.

If during this time you find yourself called to stand up for your values, the female warrior energy of Venus will support you in connecting with the lioness within. In the name of kindness, compassion and peace, her retrograde energy will encourage you to find your authentic voice, speak the truth, and stand firm in your boundaries.

Mars in Retrograde.

- **30th October 25° Gemini – 12th January 2023 08° Gemini**

When Mars moves into a retrograde motion we are asked to reassess, not only the projects, relationships, and circumstances of our external world, but also how we set about acquiring and achieving these goals.

Mars in retrograde will often highlight the role that certain emotions play in the process of manifestation, for example, anger when channeled positively through mindful considered actions creates assertiveness, however, its negative counterpart can result in aggression and frustration being directed inappropriately, towards both ourselves and others.

So, during this time, be prepared to journey inwards and reassess your needs and desires but also how you get these met… working from the inside out.

The Transpersonal Planets, Jupiter, and Saturn.

Jupiter in Retrograde.

- **28th July 08° Aries – 23rd November 28° Pisces**

A time of powerful personal growth, Jupiter in retrograde invites us on an inward quest of self-discovery seeking the knowledge and illumination that will enable us to stand in our own truth and walk our talk.

Jupiter is known as the planet of good luck and good fortune and from the perspective of manifestation, during the retrograde period we can expect to have experiences that cause us to look within and seek answers of a Spiritual nature.

The Jupiter retrograde energy helps us to forge our true values and to attune with our greater purpose and as such, during this period, windows of opportunity may open that illuminate issues from the past, including past lives, presenting us with the opportunity to find resolution and align with our true calling at this present moment of our journey.

Any internal growth and changes made during this time will then in turn, manifest outwardly and Jupiter returns to a forward flow of expansion.

Saturn in Retrograde.

- **4th June 25° Aquarius – 23rd October 18° Aquarius**

When the planet Saturn, known as Father Time and the planet of Karma, moves into retrograde, any aspects of our lives that need restructuring and reorganizing will come to a head.

We will be shown exactly what is working in our lives, alongside any aspects of our world that are not!

The lessons of Saturn can feel quite harsh as the energy calls us to account, speaking in the name of "Tough Love", however, the Saturn retrograde energy is not without reward!

The more open we are to embracing the natural evolutionary process of "weeding and pruning", letting go gracefully of anything that no longer serves us or has outlived its purpose, whether these are physical aspects of our lives or indeed any internal attitudes and beliefs, then the more smoothly these periods of profound transition will emerge.

The words "emergence" and "emergency" both come from the same source.

Saturn retrograde energy reminds us that change is both necessary and natural and that we live in a continual space of learning, not only from those wonderful experiences that fill us with joy, but also from the experiences that do not feel good and do not resonate with us.

From the perspective of manifestation, a valuable part of our ability to become consciously and actively co-creative in our lives is to be able to recognize and listen to all of our experiences, both good and bad, and to use the more challenging ones as a source of inspiration and guidance.

Rather than dwell on the negative, we can use the information from that experience to define our desires with greater clarity. This in turn opens us to receive the guidance and direction that we need to manifest those desires that resonate with us at a core level of Soul.

The Outer Planets, Uranus, Neptune, and Pluto.

The energy of the outer planets is slow moving which means that their influence is deep and penetrating creating significant growth stages with long term implications. In our individual natal charts, the positioning of these planets will not only have personal implications but will also be an indicator of generational traits.

Uranus in Retrograde.

- **20th August 2021 14° Taurus – 18th January 10° Taurus**
- **24th August 18° Taurus – 22nd January 2023 14° Taurus**

Uranus is known as the Great Awakener and the bringer of sudden changes. I always see his energy as a Lightening Spirit bringing us those thunderbolt moments where we know in no uncertain terms that something needs to change. The energy might arrive as a light bulb moment that opens a window of opportunity for change, however it can also arrive in unexpected and disruptive circumstances, shaking us out of our complacency and pushing us to take actions that free us from

When in retrograde, the impulsive and volatile energy that brings us that important and necessary wake up calls, slows down and invites us to take conscious innovative actions to forge new ways of being and living that can liberate us from limiting perspectives. This energy when harnessed is particularly relevant to establishing liberation and equality for the greater collective.

Neptune in Retrograde.

- **28th June 25° Pisces – 4th December 22° Pisces**

Neptune is the planet of creativity, dreams, and imagination and as such plays a key role in manifestation. Being so dreamy, the influence of Neptunian energy opens us to divine guidance and Spiritual illumination supporting us on our pathway of the discovery of our true calling.

However, the duality of Neptune can also create an energetic in which we struggle to hold our boundaries, lose touch with reality, or become absorbed in illusion, creating a vulnerability to those who operate through delusion and deception.

When in retrograde, the Neptunian energy calls us to get real!

Bringing a level of illumination that offers a kind of Spiritual Reality check, we can see beyond the illusions that may have previously been holding us back and use these powerful insights to initiate new pathways of creativity level to support and fuel our process of manifestation.

Pluto in Retrograde.

- **29th April 28° Capricorn – 8th October 26° Capricorn**

The energy of Pluto transforms through the natural cycle of death and re-birth and offers a powerful energetic of change. His intense volcanic energy takes us deep into the unconscious, showing us any shadows from the past that need to be released.

Pluto naturally invites us to harness the energy of personal reflection at its most powerful, bringing us an understanding of our psychological make-up so we may face our deepest issues, purify, and release, emerging afresh with greater vitality and potency.

In our process of manifestation, Pluto retrograde energy invites us to surrender to that which we are shown and to reflect on those deep inner issues that rise from the unconscious desiring change and evolution.

This is not a time to hold onto or cling to the past. If some aspect of your world seems to be coming to an end, whether internal or external, such as any outdated thinking patterns or behaviors, an inappropriate or limiting belief, or an actual situation or person, let go gracefully and allow yourself to emerge into a space of new beginnings.

Chiron and the Consciousness of Healing.

Chiron in Retrograde.

- **19th July 16° Aries – 23rd December 11° Aries**

Chiron embodies the classic architype of the wounded healer. In mythology he is depicted as half man and half beast, able to bring wisdom and to teach and heal others and yet he cannot heal himself.

Astrologically, Chiron is not a planet, but a comet, whose presence here is transient. Energetically it is said that his presence will create a rainbow bridge that will lead humanity to a higher plane of consciousness inviting us to stand in equality, not only alongside one another, but in unity with all of life. As an outer influence, his energy is slow moving and therefore can signify profound generational changes.

It is also interesting that many Tribal cultures hold legends that speak of all of the life on this planet arriving on the tail of a comet, validating the perspective that we all come from the same source and are all equal.

The retrograde energy of Chiron invites us to engage in a process of deep cleansing and release, laying the past to rest and stepping into a space of unity and higher vision. This is the kind of healing that carries the potential for us both as individuals and as a collective humanity to resolve long standing historical wounds that have spanned generations, bringing us deep and lasting healing in mind body and soul.

The Natural Turning of the Seasons

Solstices, Equinoxes, and the Festivals of the Earth

At these pivotal moments in the natural cycles of time, it is as though the Earth herself pauses for breath and the space between heaven and earth becomes fluid, translucent, and free of clutter. These shifts in time and space offer an extraordinary opportunity to achieve and access higher levels of consciousness and awareness.

During the four days either side of these powerful shifts we can often receive profound downloads of illumination, leading to an increase in our intuitive abilities. Heightening our ability to channel and connect with source energy, divine inspiration and the greater collective consciousness, people often describe a shift in perception and perspectives that free them from limiting beliefs, bringing clarity of mind and new direction.

These periods are the perfect opportunity to engage in any spiritual practice that supports your personal growth and awareness and are an ideal time to create ceremonies of appreciation, gratitude, and celebration, as part of your manifestation process.

1st February
Imbolc Northern Hemisphere – Lammas Southern Hemisphere
20th March
Spring Equinox Northern Hemisphere – Autumn Equinox Southern Hemisphere
1st May
Beltane Northern Hemisphere – Samhain Southern Hemisphere
21st June
Summer Solstice Northern Hemisphere – Winter Solstice Southern Hemisphere
1st August
Lammas Northern Hemisphere – Imbolc Southern Hemisphere
23rd September
Autumn Equinox Northern Hemisphere – Spring Equinox Southern Hemisphere
31st October
Samhain Northern Hemisphere – Beltane Southern Hemisphere
21st December
Winter Solstice Northern Hemisphere – Summer Solstice Southern Hemisphere

Journaling & Notes

The First Moon Phase of 2022

Talks with Relations - Wolf Moon – Old Moon – Cold Moon -- Birch Moon

2nd January – 31st January

Key Astrological Dates

- **2nd/3rd January – New Moon 12°19' Capricorn**
- **14th January - Mercury retrograde begins**
- **17th / 18th January - Full Moon 27°50' Cancer**
- **18th January - Uranus retrograde ends**
- **21st January – Sun enters Aquarius**
- **29th January - Venus retrograde ends**
- **1st February – New Moon 12°19' Aquarius - Lunar Imbolc/Lammas**

During this Lunar month the values and learning that underpin our personal growth and influence our creative manifestations come from the wisdom of Talks with Relations supported by the energy of Birch, inviting us to sow the seeds of new beginnings.

The wisdom of Talks with Relations taught me that everything is alive and that we are an integral part of the web of life. Her story explains how to live without judgement or competitive comparison and urges us to value difference as a source of profound learning. She teaches us that when we honor and respect all of life, we are also honoring ourselves.

During this Moon cycle I came to truly appreciate that learning to love and respect all our relations, not only our fellow human beings, but every living thing, opened new avenues of communication for me. When I learned to become still enough to truly listen, I became open to an incredible source of guidance and support.

We begin the month with the New Moon in steady solid earthy Capricorn. Get still, anchor yourself in the truth of your own real experiences and align your wishes with all that you wish to see in the world. Set intentions that make a commitment to follow through with actions that are congruent with your wishes. Living with love and respect for all of life will bring an abundance of love and respect straight back to you.

The Full Moon in Cancer, known as Old Moon, Wolf Moon and Birch Moon illuminates' pathways to new beginnings and invites us to become an observer of life and to notice what we need to change and release, so we may nurture a solid strong internal foundation of self-esteem built on true self-value and a mutuality of respect.

Honor and integrity are food for the Soul.

AMAZONITE

Amazonite.
Aligning with the First Moon Phase Talks with Relations.
Inviting respect, equality, and truth.

For me, Amazonite feels akin to the Tarot Card of Justice. It has a sense of gravity about it, calling us to stand in truth and walk a pathway of justice, equality, and fairness. And yet despite its powerful presence it radiates calm, coupled with an inner peace and an inner sense of deep wellbeing, fostering genuine self-esteem built on a foundation of honor and integrity.

It is said that the energy of Amazonite enables us to stand back and view our situation from all angles, supporting us in becoming an objective observer of life. Associated with the Heart Chakra it is said to enhance our ability to manifest through a deep connectedness with the universal love that flows through all of life.

2nd / 3rd January – New Moon in Capricorn

What an amazing start to the New Year! A New Moon sitting in a magical and flowing alignment with Uranus, the bringer of higher vision, entrepreneurial ideas and out of the box solutions!

As well as making time to list your top ten wishes of manifestation for the month ahead, you may also want to create a vision board with a clear focus on your ultimate goals for the coming year. This New Moon energy is the perfect time to turbo charge your wishes and intentions for the whole year as well as the immediate month!

A Capricorn Moon is perfect for making wishes that focus on your ambitions, goals and personal desire for success and recognition. Give yourself full permission to listen to those desires that call from your heart, as well as your mind. If you are aware of any inner blocks to your success, such as self-doubt or a lack of confidence, this is the perfect time to make wishes that support the release of any form of self-sabotaging thinking patterns or behaviors.

This is also a perfect Moon to request guidance and information to steer you in the direction of your true purpose and calling and to ask to be shown the next pragmatic and practical steps to manifest this into being.

To engage with the New Moon energy at its most powerful, be sure to write your wishes and intentions down during the 8 hours following the exact time of the New Moon in your location.

- **2nd January - Los Angeles 10.33**
- **2nd January – New York 13.33**
- **2nd January - London 18.33**
- **3rd January – Sydney 05.33**
- **3rd January – Auckland 07.33**

My Ten New Moon Wishes

1 To pay off benevure

2 To find a place where we can live the life we dream of

3 To get John's divorce over with

4 Be successful Independent celebrant

5 To increase my art sales

6 To give back to AlAnon + help others in recovery

7 To eat healthier

8

9

10

My Wishes and Dreams

My Ten New Moon Intentions

1 Starting my chosen profession as an Independent Celebrant

2 Being hired to officiate a funeral

3 Finishing perfecting my website

4 To gradually eat less meat + when I do have "grass fed" + more humane

5

6

7

8

9

10

My Intentions Are...

17th / 18th Jan - Full Moon in Cancer

Today on this Full Moon in Cancer, the Sun unites with Pluto, the planet of rebirth and transformation. A Cancer Full Moon puts us in touch with our emotions and sitting directly opposite Pluto highlights areas of life, including past issues that still carry any emotional residue bringing opportunity to cleanse and clear making way for the new. The wild passionate voice of Lilith squares strongly with illuminating Neptune emphasizing the need to listen to those deepest yearnings that speak from the heart. Mercury still in retrograde softens the overall dynamic of the day by connecting with Chiron, the wounded healer, opening channels of communication to bring healing.

Use this incredibly powerful Full Moon to identify any aspects of your emotional world that need to change and center yourself in a space of healing and regeneration making space for the new to emerge.

Each month place some rainwater or spring water in a bowl and leave it out overnight to absorb the energy of the Full Moon. Do NOT use a plastic bowl! Use glass or earthenware or any container whose fundamental ingredients come from a natural source. Collect the water afterwards and store it in a jar. You can also place your Crystals outside overnight to recharge in the powerful light of the Moon.

Use this Moon Water in any of your ceremonies where you are seeking emotional clarity, emotional release or to rebalance and strengthen your personal connection with your intuitive voice.

- **17th January - Los Angeles 15.48**
- **17th January – New York 18.48**
- **17th January - London 23.48**
- **18th January – Sydney 10.48**
- **18th January – Auckland 12.48**

My Full Moon Insights and Illuminations

The First Moon Phase

Journaling and Notes

The First Moon Phase

Journaling and Notes

Journaling and Notes

Journaling and Notes

Journaling and Notes

The First Moon Phase

Journaling and Notes

The First Moon Phase

Journaling and Notes

Journaling and Notes

Reflections from the First Moon Phase

The Second Moon Phase of 2022

Wisdom Keeper - Snow moon – Hunger Moon – Bone Moon - Rowan Moon

1st February – 1st March

Key Astrological Dates

- **1st February – New Moon 12°19' Aquarius - Lunar Imbolc/Lammas**
- **1st February - Festivals of Imbolc Northern Hemisphere - Lammas Southern Hemisphere**
- **4th February – Mercury retrograde ends**
- **16th / 17th February - Full Moon 27°59' Leo**
- **17th February – Sun enters Pisces**
- **2nd / 3rd March – New Moon 12°06' Pisces**

During this Lunar month the values and learning that underpin our personal growth and influence our creative manifestations come from the teachings of Wisdom Keeper supported by the energy of Rowan, sometimes known as the Tree of Life, and associated with courage, wisdom, and protection.

The Moon time of Wisdom Keeper brought me experiences that reminded me of the importance of keeping history alive, not in ways that cause us to remain entrenched or stuck in the past, but in ways that enable us to grow from past experiences, our own and those of our predecessors. Her teaching also deepened my acceptance of the pathways of others, with an understanding of how much we can learn from the point of views of others. On our personal journey of manifestation, when we can learn from every experience, even the most challenging ones, we become liberated from past perceptions and limitations, and can embrace the future with greater vision.

The influence of the New Moon in Aquarius aligns beautifully with these values, inviting higher vision and a life of purpose, and calling. Imbolc in the Northern Hemisphere and Lammas in the Southern Hemisphere are both festivals of celebration. Building on the foundations of our learning from January we are reminded of the commitment that we made to ourselves at the start of the year and asked to celebrate all that has brought us to this moment in time, including the learning we gain from making mistakes!

The Full Moon in Leo, known as Snow Moon, Hunger Moon, Bone Moon and Rowan Moon invites us to pause for reflection and to celebrate and value all that has brought us to this moment. Honoring memory and the wisdom of the elders, this Moon promises to illuminate the pathway that connects us with our ancestors in the dreamtime so we may discover direction and clarity of purpose.

Get into balance and feel the flow!

GREEN CALCITE

Green Calcite.
Aligning with the Second Moon Phase Wisdom Keeper.
Remembering brings healing and resolution.

Green Calcite is sometimes known as a memory stone. Aligning with the Heart Chakra and the Higher Heart Chakra, its energy supports healing within the emotional, spiritual, physical, and mental realms, thus offering opportunity to assist in the resolution of any historic or challenging memories, freeing us from the past through awareness and understanding.

I find that when I sit with this gorgeous crystal, I automatically begin to view my situation differently, and in overriding past perspectives, I can hold past memories in a far more objective and forgiving light. In meditation this crystal is said to open channels of communication with our ancestors, bringing guidance, healing, and wisdom.

31st January / 1st February – New Moon in Aquarius

This Moon of fertility marks the natural turn of the seasons and celebrates the festivals of Imbolc in the northern hemisphere and Lammas in the southern hemisphere.

The energy of an Aquarius New Moon is the perfect time to make wishes and set intentions that hold a higher vision for humanity. On our pathway of manifestation, this second New Moon of the year lends itself perfectly to build upon the foundations that we laid during the previous moon phase and to initiate wishes and intentions that bring higher love, balance, and harmony to all areas of our personal lives as well as a vision of peace for the greater collective.

Use this New Moon to make wishes that support and enhance your vision for the coming year and start to get specific about the details! If your life is feeling on track then lean into a space of excited anticipation, open yourself to receive illumination, guidance, and clarity, and dream big! If you are experiencing any form of uncertainty or apprehension about your pathway, empty your mind of pre-conceptions, lean into the higher energy of potential contribution and service, open yourself to receive guidance, and dream big!

The astro-energy at this time is insightful, with the potential to inform and illuminate, whilst simultaneously opening avenues that heal and restore balance. With the feminine energy of both Lilith and Venus making their presence known, we are called to listen and to consciously initiate actions that bring about harmonious change and transformation through equality and balance in all aspects of our lives, both inner and outer.

To engage with the New Moon energy at its most powerful, be sure to write your wishes down during the 8 hours following the exact time of the New Moon in your location.

- **31st January - Los Angeles 21.45**
- **1st February – New York 00.45**
- **1st February - London 05.45**
- **1st February – Sydney 16.45**
- **1st February – Auckland 18.45**

My Ten New Moon Wishes

1

2

3

4

5

6

7

8

9

10

My Wishes and Dreams

My Ten New Moon Intentions

1

2

3

4

5

6

7

8

9

10

My Intentions Are...

16th / 17th February - Full Moon in Leo

A Full Moon in Leo naturally invites us to embrace and enjoy exactly where we are, right here and right now. The best way to use this energy is to lean into a space of celebration, take time out to play and to recharge your batteries, whilst making a note of all that is shown to you at this time.

If any aspect of your life feels unsatisfactory then listen up! Take your passions seriously! The Leo energy helps us to identify when the desires of our ego mind are out of alignment with the desires of our heart. The influence of Leo will also support us in finding the courage to find our inner voice and to break free from inappropriate restrictions and limitations that are holding us back, both inner and outer. Likewise, if your world is feeling on track then surf the waves and go with the flow!

The dynamics of this particular Leo Full Moon have an expansive quality with the potential for sudden and unexpected opportunities to show up, and also marks the beginning of a period of incoming astro-energy that supports a flow of change and evolution. Either way, if you are shown an opening or offered an opportunity then lean into the courageous lion or lioness within and seize the moment!

Each month place some rainwater or spring water in a bowl and leave it out overnight to absorb the energy of the Full Moon. Do NOT use a plastic bowl! Use glass or earthenware or any container whose fundamental ingredients come from a natural source. Collect the water afterwards and store it in a jar.

Use this Moon Water in ceremonies of celebration or in situations where you are seeking courage.

- **16th February - Los Angeles 08.56**
- **16th February – New York 11.56**
- **16th February - London 16.56**
- **17th February – Sydney 03.56**
- **17th February – Auckland 05.56**

My Full Moon Insights and Illuminations

The Second Moon Phase

Journaling and Notes

The Second Moon Phase

Journaling and Notes

Journaling and Notes

Journaling and Notes

The Second Moon Phase

Journaling and Notes

Journaling and Notes

Journaling and Notes

Journaling and Notes

Reflections from the Second Moon Phase

The Third Moon Phase of 2022

Weighs the Truth – Worm Moon – Sap Moon – Wind Moon - Ash Moon

2nd March – 31st March

Key Astrological Dates

- **2nd / 3rd March – New Moon 12°06' Pisces**
- **18th March - Full Moon 27°39' Virgo**
- **20th March - Spring Equinox Northern Hemisphere – Autumn Equinox Southern Hemisphere**
- **21st March – Sun enters Aries**
- **1st April - New Moon 11°30' Aries**

During this Lunar month the values and learning that underpin our personal growth and influence our creative manifestations come from the wisdom of Weighs the Truth supported by the energy of Ash, who like a torch bearer, reaches tall and straight, holding the light and calling for the truth to be seen and heard. The energy of the Equinox signals a time of equal day and night, calling us to value the shadows as well as the light, it is often in passing through the darkness that we discover our greatest learning.

During the Moon time of Weighs the Truth several situations came into my world that required me to stand strong and to observe with compassion, whilst looking more deeply and asking why? To find answers, I needed to ask questions. Why do we do what we do and what drives us to act in ways that are unhelpful or damaging to ourselves or to others?

Building on the lessons and learning from the previous Lunar cycle of remembering and learning from the past, Weighs the Truth invites us to learn to evaluate circumstances in the here and now with compassion, and to take the time to build our awareness of all that has contributed to the current situation before deciding how best to respond. In my own world to find the best way forwards evaluate not only what was needed right now in the present time, but also consider the longer-term implications of my decisions and find solutions that would benefit everyone involved, and also the wider community.

The dynamics of the New Moon in Pisces are particularly favorable for higher vision and out of the box solutions so clarity of direction for your New Moon wishes and intentions may arrive in unexpected ways opening avenues for adjustment, course correction and new directions.

The Full Moon in Virgo, also known as Worm Moon, Sap Moon, Wind Moon, and Ash Moon, brings the prefect energetic to review and attend to the details, seeing every aspect of a situation before diligently following through with actions that support powerful transformation for the benefit of all.

LABRADORITE

Labradorite.
Aligning with the Third Moon Phase Weighs the Truth.
A pivotal month of transformation.

Labradorite is known as a Stone of Transformation and is said to bring the wearer strength and perseverance, its energy heightening Spiritual connections whilst grounding and strengthening trust in both ourselves and the Universe. It is known as a 'revealer' in that it shows us the Truth behind the illusion and so cuts through the concepts of our limited ego mind.

I find this stone aids and enhances my creativity helping to bring focus and channel energy into conscious, direct actions of manifestation.

2nd / 3rd March - New Moon in Pisces

If you were only going to use one Moon of the Year to set wishes and intentions then this is the one! With the energy of Uranus, the bringer of change, innovation, and entrepreneurialism, in absolute flow with this beautiful New Moon in Pisces, be sure to take advantage this powerful astrological collaboration. The stunning dynamics of this New Moon in Pisces invites your wishes to roll in like waves lapping gently on the shore. The tide is coming in and even though the waves are gentle, their forward motion is powered by the natural forces of the ocean tides.

As well as setting new wishes and intentions, use the flowing energy of this New Moon to reinforce any existing longer-term dreams and goals, inviting divine guidance and assistance in your manifestations. Any adjustments and changes that you wish to initiate at this time will carry an infusion of forward motion.

A Pisces New Moon naturally invites us to enter a space of dreamtime enhancing any wishes that are attuned with emotional sensitivity, inspired by the imagination, and connect our Spiritual awareness and our openness to receive divine assistance. If your wishes include career choices to make the most of the Piscean energy and choose wishes that support a career pathway that brings deep emotional fulfillment. If you have been hurt in love or relationship, this New Moon is perfect to wish for a relationship that re-establishes trust and is worthy of a deep soul connection. You may also want to include wishes that support you in letting go of confusion, habits of procrastination, or any self-defeating thinking patterns and behaviors.

To engage with the New Moon energy at its most powerful, be sure to write your wishes down during the 8 hours following the exact time of the New Moon in your location.

- **2nd March - Los Angeles 09.34**
- **2nd March – New York 12.34**
- **2nd March - London 17.34**
- **3rd March – Sydney 04.34**
- **3rd March – Auckland 06.34**

My Ten New Moon Wishes

1

2

3

4

5

6

7

8

9

10

My Ten New Moon Intentions

1

2

3

4

5

6

7

8

9

10

My Intentions Are...

18th March - Full Moon in Virgo

Whether you are reaching some form of completion, birthing something new into the world, or moving into the next phase of an ongoing project/ situation/ relationship, the energy of this powerful Full Moon in Virgo is an invitation to get clear and move forwards. The dynamics of this Full Moon offers huge potential for increased levels of insight, illumination, and awareness, enabling you to scrutinize, evaluate, and take actions from a position of renewed clarity.

Wherever you are on your personal journey of manifestation, there is a wonderful flow of energy available today bringing opportunity for healing through practical action.

Areas of personal conflict, with a particular focus around themes of; the needs of others versus the needs of ourselves; self-care or care of others; inappropriate levels of obligation versus realistic support of others; etc.. could well surface at this time with a call to address any imbalances both internally and externally, moving circumstances and situations into a space of transformation, completion, and re-birth.

If you are struggling to listen to your deeper feelings and/or to consider your own needs, please do remind yourself…

"Self-care is NOT an act of selfishness… it is an act of consciousness!"

Each month place some rainwater or spring water in a bowl and leave it out overnight to absorb the energy of the Full Moon. Do NOT use a plastic bowl! Use glass or earthenware or any container whose fundamental ingredients come from a natural source. Collect the water afterwards and store it in a jar. Use this Moon Water in any of your ceremonies that call for attention to detail and promote actions to heal, restore and rebalance.

- **18th March - Los Angeles 00.17**
- **18th March – New York 03.17**
- **18th March - London 07.17**
- **18th March – Sydney 18.17**
- **18th March – Auckland 20.17**

My Full Moon Insights and Illuminations

The Third Moon Phase

Journaling and Notes

The Third Moon Phase

Journaling and Notes

Journaling and Notes

The Third Moon Phase

Journaling and Notes

Journaling and Notes

Journaling and Notes

Journaling and Notes

The Third Moon Phase

Journaling and Notes

Reflections from the Third Moon Phase

The Fourth Moon Phase of 2022

Looks Far Woman – Pink Moon – Planters Moon – Alder Moon

1st April – 29th April

Key Astrological Dates

- **31st March / 1st April - New Moon 11°30' Aries**
- **16th / 17th April - Full Moon 26°45' Libra**
- **21st April – Sun enters Taurus**
- **29th April - Pluto retrograde begins**
- **30th April - New Moon 10°27' Taurus – Partial Solar Eclipse**

During this Lunar month the values and learning that underpin our personal growth and influence our creative manifestations come from the teachings of the Clan Mother, Looks Far Woman supported by the energy of Alder. Sometimes known as the Goddess tree, Alder is associated with strength, determination, protection, discernment, and confidence.

Looks Far Woman is a seer and visionary and during this Moon phase I found myself presented with many signs, signals, and synchronicities that gave me an opportunity to trust my own real experiences and learn to recognize and believe in the guidance I was being shown. Balancing the need to look into the future with the importance of being fully present and grounded in the now, the story of Looks Far Woman encouraged and inspired me to believe in possibility.

In terms of manifestation this is a powerful month of fertility. Following the growth of the third Moon phase in March where we learned to look beyond the obvious and gain understanding of cause and effect, this new phase of Lunar influence opens doorways of spiritual illumination that establish and renew faith, trust, and love.

The overall astro-dynamics of the New Moon in Aries invites us to believe in our dreams and to invest in wishes and intentions that honor our faith. The Full Moon in Libra, also known as Pink Moon, Planters Moon and Alder Moon, brings balanced perspectives and an opportunity to view any situation through the eyes of love, fostering healing and forgiveness.

ANGELITE

Angelite.
Aligning with the Fourth Moon Phase Looks Far Woman.
Trust, faith, and connection with the divine.

Angelite is an extremely high vibrational stone that just emanates peace and tranquility. Attuning us to a higher frequency it is said to create a direct channel of communication with our guardian angels and has been known to initiate and stimulate the emergence of psychic gifts and mediumship.

It is also used in healing to facilitate the rebirthing process by opening the way for spiritual inspiration, creating opportunity for psychic channeling that links us with a higher vision and a greater universal consciousness.

31st March / 1st April - New Moon in Aries

A New moon in Aries naturally supports wishes and intentions that focus on ourselves supporting personal growth, self-discovery, courage and authenticity, and new beginnings.

The Lunar energy today emphasizes the potential for healing conversations, whether with others or within ourselves so if you suffer from a debilitating inner critic this is a perfect New Moon to set wishes to easily overcome any form of internal negative dialogue.

The expansive energy of Jupiter sits with spiritual Neptune so if you are searching to find your calling or needing spiritual guidance to enhance the next steps on your pathway of conscious manifestation this is the ideal New Moon to wish for signs and signals to show you the way.

Masculine Mars and feminine Venus sit either side of the structuring energy of karmic Saturn, also connecting beautifully with the wild untamed feminine energy of Lilith. This is a perfect dynamic to focus on New Moon wishes that seek to balance and align your practical needs with your deepest desires.

In your New Moon ceremonies write down your 10 wishes and open yourself to receive the guidance that you need to highlight the next steps on your pathway of manifestation.

To engage with the New Moon energy at its most powerful, be sure to write your wishes down during the 8 hours following the exact time of the New Moon in your location.

- **31st March - Los Angeles 23.24**
- **1st April – New York 02.24**
- **1st April - London 07.24**
- **1st April – Sydney 17.24**
- **1st April – Auckland 19.24**

My Ten New Moon Wishes

1

2

3

4

5

6

7

8

9

10

My Wishes and Dreams

My Ten New Moon Intentions

1

2

3

4

5

6

7

8

9

10

My Intentions Are...

16th / 17th April – Full Moon in Libra

A Full Moon in Libra will always call us to find balance, harmony, and healing, particularly within relationship. The astro-energy of this Full Moon brings an interesting and very strong set of dynamics. Both the Moon and the Sun square with Pluto, calling for the transformation of any aspects of our world, both inner and outer that are in need of a makeover. Any circumstances or situations that we have been suppressing or denying may well surface or come to a head at this time, and with purpose!

However, the energy of the Moon and Sun also flow in harmony with Saturn supporting restructure with ease and flow. So, any situations that we have been investing in and manifesting may also come to a head, either in their completion or at a particular stage of their development, ready for the next phase and chapter to begin.

Overall, with Venus communicating well with both the great communicator Mercury and the great awakener Uranus, even though the dynamics are not without tension, particularly in any areas where we are needing to find balance there is a wonderful flow of energy available to move circumstances and situations into a space of transformation, completion, and re-birth.

Each month place some rainwater or spring water in a bowl and leave it out overnight to absorb the energy of the Full Moon. Do NOT use a plastic bowl! Use glass or earthenware or any container whose fundamental ingredients come from a natural source. Collect the water afterwards and store it in a jar.

Use the Moon Water in any of your ceremonies that support you in finding balance and speaking your truth.

- **16th April - Los Angeles 11.54**
- **16th April – New York 14.54**
- **17th April - London 19.54**
- **17th April – Sydney 04.54**
- **17th April – Auckland 06.54**

My Full Moon Insights and Illuminations

The Fourth Moon Phase

Journaling and Notes

Journaling and Notes

Journaling and Notes

Journaling and Notes

Journaling and Notes

Journaling and Notes

Journaling and Notes

Journaling and Notes

Reflections from the Fourth Moon Phase

The Fifth Moon Phase of 2022

Listening Woman – Flower Moon – Budding Moon – Willow Moon

30th April – 29th May

Key Astrological Dates

- **30th April / 1st May - New Moon 10°27’ Taurus – Partial Solar Eclipse**
- **1st May - Festival of Beltane Northern Hemisphere – Samhain Southern Hemisphere**
- **10th May – Mercury retrograde begins**
- **15th / 16th May - Full Moon 25°17’ Scorpio – Total Lunar Eclipse – Blood Moon**
- **22nd May – Sun enters Gemini**
- **30th May - New Moon 09°03’ Gemini**

During this Lunar month the values and learning that underpin our personal growth and influence our creative manifestations come from the teachings of Listening Woman supported by the energy of Willow connecting us with our deepest emotions. Tuning in with the energy of Beltane in the Northern Hemisphere and Samhain in the Southern Hemisphere, both festivals of Fire, there is a definite flavor of passion and emotional intensity in the ethers.

The Moon time of Listening Woman focused my attention on the details of my thoughts and words and made me realize how big a part they play in the constant flow of our manifestations. Her story made me step back from the drama that our ego mind can so easily create or buy into, and to listen to what was being said, and also when necessary, to what was not being said.

The learning of this Moon phase revolutionized my ability to develop healthy discernment and through well informed listening with recognition and ownership of my personal choices and responses I started to manage and maintain my boundaries with strength and confidence.

The New Moon eclipse in earthy Taurus helps us to unearth and heal any insecurities that stop us from hearing the truth and the dynamic Full Moon Eclipse in Scorpio, also known as Flower Moon, Budding Moon and Willow Moon connects us with deep emotions, illuminating hidden depths and revealing aspects of ourselves and others that are often kept under wraps.

There is much opportunity in this Moon phase for heightened levels of awareness and the revealing of karmic patterns, with an opportunity to release and transform.

AGATE BLUE LACE

Agate Blue Lace.
Aligning with the Fifth Moon Phase Listening Woman.
Look beyond the obvious, there is a story to be heard.

Said to improve concentration, perception, and mental sharpness the powerfully transformative energy of Agate eliminates and transforms negativity, energizing a sense of safety and security through the holding of firm boundaries.

Cleansing us from the inside out and reaching into our Aura, Blue Lace Agate not only carries all of the fundamental qualities of Agate but seems to add an additional energy of peace and tranquility. Said to sooth the voice and release any restrictive energy around the throat Chakra, this powerful little stone supports us in finding a voice to express thoughts and feelings with a calm and mindful clarity.

30th April / 1st May - New Moon Eclipse in Taurus

The energy of a Solar Eclipse is often associated with a surge of creative possibilities, although these may not always arrive in the form that we were expecting! The dynamics of this New Moon Eclipse is perfect to consciously focus on the relationship between your New Moon Wishes and your New moon Intentions! There is a difference between New Moon Wishes and New Moon Intentions and when we use the energy of both, in balance and harmony, the collaboration of the two strengthens the potential support that is available to us at the beginning of every new Lunar cycle.

This New Moon in Taurus makes a very dynamic and positive connection with the fiery, go-getting energy of Mars. We also see harmonious, balanced Venus and expansive, optimistic Jupiter joining forces and creating a flowing dynamic with the transformative energy of Pluto.

You may well find that certain stages of your personal manifestations suddenly shift. Some may suddenly bloom and emerge, birthing into the world, creating space for a new cycle of evolution and manifestation. Others may suddenly gather momentum and begin to move forwards, finding shape and form. Others may reach a certain stage of development highlighting whatever is needed for the next surge of input and action.

It's time to take action!

In your New Moon ceremonies write down your 10 wishes and open yourself to receive the guidance that you need to highlight the next steps on your pathway of manifestation. To engage with the New Moon energy at its most powerful, be sure to write your wishes down during the 8 hours following the exact time of the New Moon in your location.

- **30th April - Los Angeles 13.27**
- **30th April – New York 16.27**
- **30th April - London 21.27**
- **1st May – Sydney 06.27**
- **1st May – Auckland 08.27**

My Ten New Moon Wishes

1

2

3

4

5

6

7

8

9

10

My Wishes and Dreams

My Ten New Moon Intentions

1

2

3

4

5

6

7

8

9

10

My Intentions Are…

15th / 16th May - Full Moon Eclipse in Scorpio

A Full Moon in Scorpio will tend to illuminate the shadows, inviting us to dive deep and look at ourselves and our situations with honesty. As the saying goes, when in deep water, become a diver! The Scorpio energy supports the letting go of things that no longer serve us, making room for transformation, renewal and rebirth.

This particular Full Moon Eclipse brings some very strong dynamics all of which invite us to peel back the layers and dive deep into a space of profound awareness. Eclipses are associated with our Karmic journey and are said to create an energetic rift or portal that can assist in connecting us with our purpose and calling in this present lifetime. Today our beautiful Moon sits with the North Node also bringing heightened awareness of the impact of our actions, past, present, and future. As always at a Full Moon she sits opposite the Sun and both in turn square up with Saturn, sometimes known as Father Time and the planet of Karmic lessons.

If you are in anyway unsure of your calling or are seeking illumination and guidance to inform your pathway at this time then this powerful Full Moon Eclipse is the perfect time to dedicate structured time to meditate or engage in Shamanic journeying. And if you find yourself dreaming prolifically, keep a dream journal as much may be revealed.

Each month place some rainwater or spring water in a bowl and leave it out overnight to absorb the energy of the Full Moon. Do NOT use a plastic bowl! Use glass or earthenware or any container whose fundamental ingredients come from a natural source. Collect the water afterwards and store it in a jar.

Use the Moon Water in any of your ceremonies that invite deep enquiry, transformation, and re-birth.

- **15th May - Los Angeles 21.13**
- **16th May – New York 00.13**
- **16th May - London 05.13**
- **16th May – Sydney 14.13**
- **16th May – Auckland 16.13**

My Full Moon Insights and Illuminations

The Fifth Moon Phase

Journaling and Notes

Journaling and Notes

Journaling and Notes

The Fifth Moon Phase

Journaling and Notes

Journaling and Notes

Journaling and Notes

Journaling and Notes

Journaling and Notes

Reflections from the Fifth Moon Phase

The Sixth Moon Phase of 2022

Storyteller – Strawberry Moon – Rose Moon – Hawthorn Moon

30th May – 28th June

Key Astrological Dates

- **30th May - New Moon 09°03' Gemini**
- **3rd June – Mercury retrograde ends**
- **4th June – Saturn retrograde begins**
- **14th June – Super Full Moon 23°24' Sagittarius**
- **21st June - Summer Solstice Northern Hemisphere – Winter Solstice Southern Hemisphere**
- **22nd June – Sun enters Cancer**
- **28th June – Neptune retrograde begins**
- **29th June - New moon 07°22' Cancer**

During this Lunar month the values and learning that underpin our personal growth and influence our creative manifestations come from the wisdom of Storyteller supported by Hawthorn, whose energy aligns with protection, teaching us that personal strength stems from the recognition of our own power and the ability to take charge of this, without any need to exert power over others.

The New Moon in Gemini invites us to evaluate our options and to view all sides of the story before making our choices and decisions and the Super Full Moon in Sagittarius also known as Strawberry Moon, Rose Moon and Hawthorn Moon, illuminates' areas of our lives that seek change, and through embracing an attitude of gratitude, opens avenues of hope and optimism for the future. Followed by the natural turning point of the Solstice, this Lunar phase invites us to pause and observe the timeline of our lives, reflecting on our past, our present and our future and the empowerment that this awareness brings.

During the Moon time of Storyteller, I found myself dreaming about and reflecting on my own history and I began to appreciate that everything that had happened in my life had formed and established who I have become and the values that I hold so dear. It also became very clear to me that whilst I have no control over the pathways of others, I can view their actions with compassion.

If I don't like someone's actions, it is empowering to remember that I do not know what brought them to this point in their journey, and if their actions are causing damage, then I can be almost certain that they are still carrying unresolved issues from their past… however, it is not my responsibility to fix them or try to direct them. Their choices are their own.

Likewise, if I don't like any aspects of my own life or I am still living through any outdated assumptions, attitudes, or perspectives that are rooted in the past, then I can change this. Storyteller highlights the lessons that our life circumstances bring us and through awareness with compassion, invites us to grow beyond these limitations.

LAPIS LAZULI

Lapis Lazuli.
Aligning with the Sixth Moon Phase Storyteller.
What is your story?

Be the change that you wish to see in the world! Stand in your truth and find your voice! This magnificent stone radiates the energy of the Spiritual Warrior striving to walk a pathway of authenticity.

Lapis Lazuli is a powerful stone of self-expression. Said to reveal our inner truth through self-awareness, this extraordinary stone is said to encourage us to uphold honesty and integrity whilst observing ourselves and others through the eyes of compassion.

30th May - New Moon in Gemini

A New Moon in Gemini will naturally invite wishes and intentions that support better and fluent communication, clear thinking and speaking, and the calming of mental energy.

Our beautiful New Moon connects with expansive Jupiter and the masculine go-getting warrior energy of Mars. They both in turn square up with the deep passionate callings of Lilith, so if you feel restless or uneasy, take this seriously and make time to listen to the source of these feelings. Have that conversation with yourself and take some time to internally unpack.

If you feel the need to have a voice today and to speak your truth or you need to find a clarity of thought or direction the energy of a Gemini New moon naturally invites curiosity and brings the inspiration we need to create change and the overall dynamics of this New Moon favors the expansion of ideas and having your voice through creative expression.

Weigh up all of the different possibilities and use your New Moon wishes to ask for clarity as to the best option for you at this moment in time.

In your New Moon ceremonies write down your 10 wishes and open yourself to receive the guidance that you need to highlight the next steps on your pathway of manifestation.

To engage with the New Moon energy at its most powerful, be sure to write your wishes down during the 8 hours following the exact time of the New Moon in your location.

- **30th May - Los Angeles 04.30**
- **30th May – New York 07.30**
- **30th May - London 12.30**
- **30th May – Sydney 21.30**
- **30th May – Auckland 23.30**

My Ten New Moon Wishes

1

2

3

4

5

6

7

8

9

10

My Wishes and Dreams

My Ten New Moon Intentions

1

2

3

4

5

6

7

8

9

10

My Intentions Are...

14th June - Super Full Moon in Sagittarius

A Full Moon in Sagittarius will naturally help to align us with renewed enthusiasm, igniting our passions, especially in areas of life that connect us with justice, purpose, and freedom.

As we approach the turning point of the Solstice the dynamics of this Super Full Moon suggest powerful completions and potential healing with the Sagittarian influence inviting us to free ourselves from anything that may be holding us back, tie up loose ends and begin to formulate and plan for the next phase on our journey of manifestation.

The Sun, Moon and Neptune collaborate, bringing to light any areas of emotional charge that require our attention and Chiron the wounded healer, aligns with the masculine warrior energy of Mars, opening a pathway of healing to clear the way for new hope, new vision, and new optimism.

Each month place some rainwater or spring water in a bowl and leave it out overnight to absorb the energy of the Full Moon. Do NOT use a plastic bowl! Use glass or earthenware or any container whose fundamental ingredients come from a natural source. Collect the water afterwards and store it in a jar.

Use this Moon Water in any of your ceremonies of manifestation that support the letting go of inhibitions and negative thinking patterns and a realignment with hope and optimism.

- **14th June - Los Angeles 04.51**
- **14th June – New York 07.51**
- **14th June - London 12.51**
- **14th June – Sydney 21.51**
- **14th June – Auckland 23.21**

My Full Moon Insights and Illuminations

The Sixth Moon Phase

Journaling and Notes

Journaling and Notes

Journaling and Notes

The Sixth Moon Phase

Journaling and Notes

Journaling and Notes

Journaling and Notes

Journaling and Notes

Journaling and Notes

Reflections from the Sixth Moon Phase

The Seventh Moon Phase of 2022

Loves All Things – Buck Moon – Thunder Moon – Oak Moon

29th June – 27th July

Key Astrological Dates

- **29th June - New moon 07°22' Cancer**
- **13th July – Super Full Moon 21°20' Capricorn**
- **19th July – Chiron retrograde begins**
- **23rd July– Sun enters Leo**
- **28th July - New Moon 05°38' Leo**

During this Lunar month the values and learning that underpin our personal growth and influence our creative manifestations come from the teachings of the Clan Mother, Loves All Things. The energy of Oak teaches us about the circle of life and reminds us to love and appreciate the present and value the abundance of all that we have, right now.

The astro-energy in July sees a dynamic month with a push and pull of activity that alternates between internal growth and external growth, reminding us that change always starts from within and with five of the major planets all in retrograde by the end of the month, we might expect our external manifestations to slow down and to see a shift towards any inner work that is needed. The New Moon in Cancer honors the teachings of Loves All Things, inviting us to nurture our dreams and surround our hopes for the future in Love.

During this Moon time the events in my life perfectly mirrored so much of the learning of Loves All Things. Hearing her story of love and loss, I was able to navigate a very close loss in my own life, without losing faith or trust in life, if anything, my appreciation of life, especially the really tiny things that can so easily go unnoticed, was massively enhanced and I was able to approach love and see love in a very different way.

The Super Full Moon in earthy Capricorn also known as Buck Moon, Thunder Moon and Oak Moon, reminds us to get present and invites a very real and very honest review of ourselves and our circumstances. For me, the Moon time of Loves All Things offers us a return to Love in every aspect of our lives with a personal liberation that comes from this level of Soul growth. Through her teachings of fostering the best in ourselves and others through nurture and validation, rather than a focus on faults and mistakes through criticism and judgment, with acceptance and forgiveness of both myself and others I gained a much deeper sense of self-respect.

MOONSTONE

Moonstone.
Aligning with the Seventh Moon Phase Loves All Things.
Love Heals All.

Moonstone invites us to open our hearts and to love without judgment. It is associated with fertility and sensuality connecting us with the inner goddess that sits within us all, heightening our intuition, and clearing and cleansing our mind from any negative emotions, especially those connected to our relationships.

Used in meditation, particularly at the time of the New Moon, it is said to enhance our powers of manifestation. Moonstone brings a wonderful energy into any New Moon ceremonies associated with our dreams, wishes and desires reminding us of the Miracles that surround us and of the infinite support of Spirit and the Universe.

28th / 29th June - New Moon in Cancer

The energy of a Cancer New Moon will naturally invite us to focus on wishes that connect to our sense of belonging, our home, and our family.

The dynamics of this particular Moon are fascinating and embrace feminine energy at its most powerful! Our beautiful Moon sits with feminine voice of Lilith and their combined energy is then expanded by Jupiter who in turn flows harmoniously with the balanced feminine energy of Venus.

These dynamics suggest that anything and everything in our worlds that are in balance and in alignment will flow into their highest form.

Likewise, anything and everything that resists or works against truth, fairness, equality, and the settling of past injustices will call… or indeed perhaps shout… for our attention!

If you are someone who feels particularly vulnerable during times of change and transition the energy of this New Moon will lend itself beautifully to wishes that release you from anxiety and insecurity, inviting stability and emotional strength and resilience and if you have been hurt in the past, this is an ideal New Moon to set wishes to invite new and harmonious relationships into your life.

In your New Moon ceremonies write down your 10 wishes and open yourself to receive the guidance that you need to highlight the next steps on your pathway of manifestation.

To engage with the New Moon energy at its most powerful, be sure to write your wishes down during the 8 hours following the exact time of the New Moon in your location.

- **28th June - Los Angeles 19.52**
- **28th June – New York 22.52**
- **29th June - London 03.52**
- **29th June – Sydney 12.52**
- **29th June – Auckland 14.52**

My Ten New Moon Wishes

1

2

3

4

5

6

7

8

9

10

My Ten New Moon Intentions

1

2

3

4

5

6

7

8

9

10

My Intentions Are...

13th / 14th July – Super Full Moon in Capricorn

This promises to be a very dynamic Super Full Moon! The enhanced influence of a Super Full Moon brings illumination and flowing within the influence of Capricorn, invites practical, pragmatic, review, with a realistic summing up and realistic appraisal.

With three of the big influencers, Pluto, Saturn, and Neptune all now in retrograde, retrospective reflections are invited, and as our beautiful Moon joins forces with Pluto these reflections may well open pathways to transformation, re-birth, and renewal.

This powerful Lunar energy is also added to by the great awakener Uranus, who collaborates with the karmic energy of the North Node, creating the energetic potential to bring new perspectives, out of the box solutions and unexpected new opportunities!

Each month place some rainwater or spring water in a bowl and leave it out overnight to absorb the energy of the Full Moon. Do NOT use a plastic bowl! Use glass or earthenware or any container whose fundamental ingredients come from a natural source. Collect the water afterwards and store it in a jar.

Use this Moon Water in any of your ceremonies of manifestation to support clear pragmatic steps in following your calling, purpose, and destiny.

- **13rd July - Los Angeles 11.37**
- **13rd July – New York 14.37**
- **13th July - London 19.37**
- **14th July – Sydney 04.37**
- **14th July – Auckland 06.37**

My Full Moon Insights and Illuminations

Journaling and Notes

Journaling and Notes

Journaling and Notes

Journaling and Notes

Journaling and Notes

Journaling and Notes

The Seventh Moon Phase

Journaling and Notes

Reflections from the Seventh Moon Phase

The Eighth Moon Phase of 2022

She Who Heals – Sturgeon Moon – Green Corn Moon – Holly Moon

28th July -26th August

Key Astrological Dates

- **28th / 29th July - New Moon 05°38' Leo**
- **28th July – Jupiter retrograde begins**
- **1st August - Festival of Lammas Northern Hemisphere – Imbolc Southern Hemisphere**
- **11th / 12th August - Full Moon 19°21' Aquarius**
- **24th August – Sun enters Virgo**
- **24th August - Uranus retrograde begins**
- **27th August - New moon 08°03' Virgo**

During this Lunar cycle the values and learning that underpin our personal growth and influence our creative manifestations come from the wisdom and teachings of She Who Heals, supported by the energy of Holly, which is associated with rites of passage, transition, and the circle of life, death, and re-birth.

The New Moon in Leo heralds a Lunar phase of healing and calls us to validate our progress and to celebrate how far we have come and where we are right now. August honors this celebration with Lammas in the Northern Hemisphere and Imbolc in the Southern Hemisphere. Both are festivals that validate growth whilst also recognizing the need to nurture with patience and consistency if we are to bring in a full and prosperous harvest at a later date.

In perfect alignment with the teachings of She Who Heals, in pausing to notice, celebrate and review, I found that during this Moon cycle, I became aware of old wounds that I had never quite managed to resolve and put to rest. Situations arrived in my world that peeled back the layers, showing me clearly what I needed to let go of, release, and move beyond. In clearing and healing, mind, body, and soul, I found renewed positivity and vitality. I came to understand that periods of transition and growth are always accompanied by the process of loss, healing, and re-birth.

The magical teachings of She Who Heals emphasizes the gift of self-responsibility, supporting us to take charge of our own negativity and change our dialogue and thinking patterns into thoughts of health, positivity, and love, enabling us to heal ourselves, and to become a channel of healing for others as well.

The Full Moon in Aquarius also known as Sturgeon Moon, Green Corn Moon and Holly Moon, aligns beautifully with these teachings, inviting higher vision and perspectives that honor the collective as well as the individual.

Orange Calcite.
Aligning with the Eighth Moon Phase She Who Heals.
Healing and renewed vitality.

Known as the 'Enhancement Stone', Orange Calcite, like other calcites is said to have powerful healing attributes. Associated with the energy of the Sun and the element of Fire, this stunning crystal is said to realign us with renewed vitality, energizing our primary life force.

In my own experience, I can recommend that if you are struggling to feel the confidence to step into your fullest potential or need some assistance to remove inner blocks to discovering and fulfilling your life's purpose then this stunning crystal brings just the energy needed to support you in this process.

28th / 29th July - New Moon in Leo

A New Moon in Leo naturally lends itself to wishes that focus on creativity, love and romance, playfulness, generosity, and fun. The energy of a Leo New Moon also supports us in making wishes that enhance our personal passions, our leadership qualities, bring us enthusiasm and determination and encourage the building of our confidence and individual self-expression.

The strongest connection of this New Moon in Leo is a beautiful trine with expansive, optimistic Jupiter, who is literally about to move into a retrograde motion, and with the great awakener Uranus and the karmic energy of the North Node holding their conjunction, get present... and consciously choose to hold a mindset of possibility.

The outgoing energy of Leo invites celebration and affirmation so in preparation for your New Moon wishes and intentions, take time to acknowledge and validate where you are right now, and all that has led you to this point in your life. Center yourself in gratitude for all of the learning and the life experiences that have made you who you are. And now... with the turbo charged energy of gratitude, focus on your wishes and intentions for the life that you are manifesting!

In your New Moon ceremonies write down your 10 wishes and open yourself to receive the guidance that you need to highlight the next steps on your pathway of manifestation.

To engage with the New Moon energy at its most powerful, be sure to write your wishes down during the 8 hours following the exact time of the New Moon in your location.

- **28th July - Los Angeles 10.54**
- **28th July – New York 13.54**
- **28th July - London 18.54**
- **29th July – Sydney 03.54**
- **29th July – Auckland 05.54**

My Ten New Moon Wishes

1

2

3

4

5

6

7

8

9

10

My Ten New Moon Intentions

1

2

3

4

5

6

7

8

9

10

My Intentions Are...

11th / 12th August - Full Moon in Aquarius

The Full Moon in Aquarius naturally opens a space of insight and higher vision, to bring clarity and point us in the right direction. With so many planets in retrograde take the opportunity to meditate into a space of possibility and be open to receive the guidance needed to highlight new pathways of conscious activity to bring your visions of manifestation into form.

Today's Full Moon in Aquarius aligns with the retrograde energy of Saturn, our great teacher and bringer of life lessons, inviting us to re-evaluate, reconsider, and restructure. Changeable Uranus, who also rules Aquarius, remains firmly attached to the North Node, opposite the South Node, suggesting that events will bring us what we need, (though not necessarily what we want,) all in the service of keeping us on track and aligning us with our purpose and calling.

With Mars adding some fiery input this looks to be an exciting Full Moon with the opportunity to celebrate and validate whilst also letting go of any situations, attitudes, and perceptions from the past that may have been getting in the way or hindering our progress in stepping up and becoming the very best version of ourselves in all aspects of our lives.

Each month place some rainwater or spring water in a bowl and leave it out overnight to absorb the energy of the Full Moon. Do NOT use a plastic bowl! Use glass or earthenware or any container whose fundamental ingredients come from a natural source. Collect the water afterwards and store it in a jar.

Use this Moon Water in any of your ceremonies of manifestation when you are seeking clarity of direction and furthering your purpose and calling.

- **11th August - Los Angeles 18.35**
- **11th August – New York 21.35**
- **12th August - London 02.35**
- **12th August – Sydney 11.35**
- **12th August – Auckland 13.35**

My Full Moon Insights and Illuminations

Journaling and Notes

Journaling and Notes

Journaling and Notes

Journaling and Notes

Journaling and Notes

Journaling and Notes

Journaling and Notes

Journaling and Notes

Reflections from the Eighth Moon Phase

The Ninth Moon Phase of 2022

Setting Sun Woman – Harvest Moon – Corn Moon – Hazel Moon

27th August – 24th September

Key Astrological Dates

- **27th August - New moon 08°03' Virgo**
- **10th September Mercury retrograde begins**
- **10th September - Full Moon 17°40' Pisces**
- **23rd September - Autumn Equinox Northern Hemisphere – Spring Equinox Southern Hemisphere**
- **24th September – Sun enters Libra**
- **25th September - New Moon 02°48' Libra**

During this Lunar month the values and learning that underpin our personal growth and influence our creative manifestations come from the teachings of Setting Sun Woman who is the keeper of tomorrows goals and dreams. The energy of Hazel supports the learning of this Lunar cycle bringing wisdom and inspiration through the magic of divination and prophecy.

For me this period marks a culmination of the growth and evolution throughout the year. The turning point of the Equinox highlights a period of natural transition and as I process and move beyond the extraordinary healing gifted in the previous Lunar phase, areas of discord that had previously held me back are finding closure, and like an internal harvest of renewed potential, little by little, clarity of direction filters into my mind.

Whilst I know that there is always more work to be done in the ever-evolving spiral of life, right now, as peace of mind increasingly comes more readily, I find myself humbled in gratitude for all that I have, and mindful to consider my future desires carefully with an awareness that stretches beyond my own lifetime and into the lives of future of generations.

With a profound sense of internal peace, I look forwards and anticipate the dreams and promise of the future yet to come. Beginning with the New moon in Virgo this phase honors perseverance and a diligent state of mind, being thoughtful to preserve and conserve for a future that stretches beyond ourselves and our own needs and desires. The Full Moon in Pisces also known as

Harvest Moon, Corn Moon and Hazel Moon, opens channels of divine guidance lighting the way to a better future and a better humanity.

SELENITE

Selenite.
Aligning with the Ninth Moon Phase Setting Sun Woman.
A Moon phase of profound gratitude!

Selenite draws its name came from Selene, the Greek Goddess of the Moon, and just as the Moon gathers light from the Sun and redistributes it across the Earth, so too Selenite literally embodies and radiates light.

This magical and illuminating crystal can be used for healing in its own right or used with other crystals. I personally keep several Selenite sticks and much as I would put my crystals out overnight to re-charge at the Full Moon, I use my selenite sticks to re-charge the energy of my other crystals.

Associated with the alignment of the third eye, crown and etheric chakras, this powerful crystal is a must for anyone seeking to connect with their Guides and Angels, also known as an Abundance Stone, perhaps a reflection of its generous and giving nature, it is said to raise our awareness and connect us with our higher self.

27th August - New Moon in Virgo

A New Moon in Virgo lends itself well to areas of our lives that involve our physical health and wellbeing, our careers and workplace, and our ability to be organized and efficient. It also connects to our capacity be discerning within our relationships and hold our boundaries.

The overall energetics of this New Moon support dynamic action, so to best align with the energy of the day and utilize its fullest potential, make a commitment to yourself to honor the validity of your New Moon wishes and declare your commitment to follow through with your New Moon intentions. Use this New Moon Energy to wish for the perfect work life balance that allows you to uphold a consistent flow of healthy energy that brings wellness in both mind, body, and soul.
If you are looking to manifest a new career pathway use the energy of this New Moon to set wishes that invite a career position that aligns you with your greatest contribution.

If you are experiencing any form of dissatisfaction, conflict, or challenge, particularly at work with either managers or subordinates, use this New Moon to wish for a balanced resolution that values all parties.

If you are someone who is crippled by perfectionism and carries a raging inner critic, use this New Moon to make wishes that ask to release these internal thinking patterns with ease.

In your New Moon ceremonies write down your 10 wishes and open yourself to receive the guidance that you need to highlight the next steps on your pathway of manifestation.

To engage with the New Moon energy at its most powerful, be sure to write your wishes down during the 8 hours following the exact time of the New Moon in your location.

- **27th August - Los Angeles 01.16**
- **27th August – New York 04.16**
- **27th August - London 09.16**
- **27th August – Sydney 18.16**
- **27th August – Auckland 20.16**

My Ten New Moon Wishes

1

2

3

4

5

6

7

8

9

10

My Ten New Moon Intentions

1

2

3

4

5

6

7

8

9

10

My Intentions Are...

10th September - Full Moon in Pisces

The Full Moon in Pisces naturally beckons us to connect with a sense of greater meaning in our lives and our spiritual pathway. Piscean energy is often highly emotional and in terms of illuminating those aspects of our lives that need to be released this Moon can feel both liberating and/or a little overwhelming depending on our unique individual circumstances.

There is a powerful theme of transformation in the overall Lunar energy at the moment as the Moon moves closer and closer towards retrograde Neptune and the Saturn/Uranus square that dominated the year of 2021, inviting us to embrace transformation and the emergence of humanity into a new age, now aligns with the Nodes, suggesting that for the latter part of this year, we may expect an ongoing flow of potential to align our manifestations with dreams and visions of higher calling and personal purpose.

If you are in any way uncertain as to your next move forwards this is the perfect day to take time out and engage in full on meditation practice with ceremonies that invite illumination and divine guidance.

A Full Moon in Pisces will often highlight any areas of our personal world that are still entangled in any emotional residue of the past, creating a window of opportunity to cleanse, release, and heal.

Each month place some rainwater or spring water in a bowl and leave it out overnight to absorb the energy of the Full Moon. Do NOT use a plastic bowl! Use glass or earthenware or any container whose fundamental ingredients come from a natural source. Collect the water afterwards and store it in a jar.

Use this Moon Water in any of your ceremonies when you need emotional release. It is also perfect to add a power boost in ceremonies to connect with Spirit and seek guidance to manifest your calling and your higher purpose.

- **10th September - Los Angeles 02.58**
- **10th September – New York 05.58**
- **10th September - London 10.58**
- **10th September – Sydney 19.58**
- **10th September – Auckland 21.58**

My Full Moon Insights and Illuminations

Journaling and Notes

Journaling and Notes

Journaling and Notes

Journaling and Notes

Journaling and Notes

The Ninth Moon Phase

Journaling and Notes

Journaling and Notes

Journaling and Notes

Reflections from the Ninth Moon Phase

The Tenth Moon Phase of 2022

Weaves the Web – Hunters Moon – Moon of Falling Leaves – Vine Moon

25th September – 24th October

Key Astrological Dates

- **25th September - New Moon 02°48' Libra**
- **2nd October - Mercury retrograde ends**
- **8th October - Pluto retrograde ends**
- **9th October - Full Moon 16°32' Aries**
- **23rd October - Saturn retrograde ends**
- **24th October – Sun enters Scorpio**
- **25th October - New Moon 01°59' Scorpio – Partial Solar Eclipse**

During this Lunar month the values and learning that underpin our personal growth and influence our creative manifestations come from the wisdom of Weaves the Web, supported by the energy of Vine, representing strength, determination and the bonds of friendship and family.

With several planets coming out of retrograde you may notice a tangible shift in the energy. For me the Moon cycle of Weaves the Web always feels like a time to move forwards and embrace the joy of both doing and being. I feel connected to the cycle of creation and whether I am persevering to bring existing projects to fruition or sowing new seeds of creative expression, the Lunar energy of this phase seems to help me to renew my motivation and overcome any form of procrastination. There is always more growth to be had but by the time we reach this tenth Moon cycle my internal foundations feel a little bit stronger and I feel that I can walk a little bit taller.

For me this is a time to honor the balance of both giving and receiving, to share our gifts, and to expand and build the skills we need to make our dreams real and bring our manifestations into form.

The beautiful New Moon in Libra naturally supports balance, harmony, and beauty, honoring the creativity of both the divine feminine and the divine masculine that sits within us each. The Full Moon in Aries also known as Hunters Moon, Moon of Falling Leaves and Vine Moon, ignites passion bringing the enthusiasm needed to fire us up and move our creative endeavors forwards. This truly is a Moon phase that fosters manifestation in all ways.

CARNELIAN

Carnelian.
Aligning with the Tenth Moon Phase Weaves the Web.
A shift in the energy of manifestation.

Carnelian has to be one of my most favorite Raw Crystals! For me, it is one of those Crystals that does exactly what is says on the tin! The energy of Carnelian is said to restore vitality and bring motivation. Stimulating creativity, it promotes positive life choices.

A powerful crystal of vibrant energy, it is said to bring courage and create a mindset that motivates for success. If you need energy to begin a project or strength and durability to see you through to the finish line, or indeed if you are someone who struggles with a debilitating inner critic that inhibits your perseverance, then this dynamic crystal could become a great friend and ally to you.

25th / 26th September New Moon in libra

The New Moon in Libra is naturally inclined to support all aspects of balance and harmony in our lives and in our relationships.

If you are seeking to make wishes that involve the realignment of any aspect of your wellbeing this is a perfect New Moon to set wishes that realign and rebalance your Chakras, and if you are seeking long term balance and harmony within relationship and desire marriage and a union of equality then a Libra New Moon is the perfect time to set wishes in this area of your life.

The overall astro-dynamics today are absolutely loaded with opportunity and promise to add a turbo charged boost of power to our New Moon wishes and intentions.

Take full advantage of this energetic!

And if you are someone who struggles to negotiate effectively then this is an also the perfect Moon to ask for assistance in releasing any issues surrounding your own self-value and to request support to develop fluent communications and dealings with others that are fair and equal to all parties, including yourself.

In your New Moon ceremonies write down your 10 wishes and open yourself to receive the guidance that you need to highlight the next steps on your pathway of manifestation.

To engage with the New Moon energy at its most powerful, be sure to write your wishes down during the 8 hours following the exact time of the New Moon in your location.

- **25th September - Los Angeles 14.54**
- **25th September – New York 17.54**
- **25th September - London 22.54**
- **26th September – Sydney 08.54**
- **26th September – Auckland 10.54**

My Ten New Moon Wishes

1

2

3

4

5

6

7

8

9

10

My Wishes and Dreams

My Ten New Moon Intentions

1

2

3

4

5

6

7

8

9

10

My Intentions Are...

9th / 10th October - Full Moon in Aries

The Full Moon in Aries inspires us pursue our dreams with passion, illuminating those areas of our lives that are on track… as well as those that are not! The energy of an Aries Full Moon naturally lends itself to the initiation of new beginnings, bringing us the courage to step out of our comfort zone and into our fullest potential, fueling our actions with desire and motivation.

This is a Full Moon that invites us to make things happen. You may feel elated and experience a burst of renewed passion and enthusiasm, however in areas of life that feel uncertain or difficult then emotions could feel a little intense. In terms of ongoing manifestation, the overall astro-dynamics today suggest that much may be illuminated to shows us the way forwards, whether in validation of our progress or in validation of a needed change.

The Saturn/Uranus square remains exact bringing innovation and out of the box solutions that invite us both individually and collectively to call in new ways of seeing, doing, and being! All in all, the overall energy invites us to open our arms and welcome in a new and better future and be active in doing so.

Each month place some rainwater or spring water in a bowl and leave it out overnight to absorb the energy of the Full Moon. Do NOT use a plastic bowl! Use glass or earthenware or any container whose fundamental ingredients come from a natural source. Collect the water afterwards and store it in a jar.

Use this Moon Water in any of your ceremonies that are connected to initiating new beginnings or when you need courage to either step into the new, or to hold your direction with purpose and intent.

- **9th October - Los Angeles 13.54**
- **9th October – New York 16.54**
- **9th October - London 21.54**
- **10th October – Sydney 07.54**
- **10th October – Auckland 09.54**

My Full Moon Insights and Illuminations

The Tenth Moon Phase

Journaling and Notes

Journaling and Notes

Journaling and Notes

Journaling and Notes

The Tenth Moon Phase

Journaling and Notes

Journaling and Notes

Journaling and Notes

Journaling and Notes

Reflections from the Tenth Moon Phase

The Tenth Moon Phase

The Eleventh Moon Phase of 2022

Walks Tall Woman – Beaver Moon – Frost Moon – Ivy Moon

25th October – 22nd November

Key Astrological Dates

- **25th October - New Moon 01°59' Scorpio – Partial Solar Eclipse**
- **30th October – Mars retrograde begins**
- **31st October - Festival of Samhain Northern Hemisphere – Beltane Southern Hemisphere**
- **8th November - Full Moon 16°00' Taurus - Total Lunar Eclipse – Blood Moon**
- **23rd November - Jupiter retrograde ends**
- **23rd November – Sun enters Sagittarius**
- **23rd November - New Moon 01°37' Sagittarius**

During this Lunar month the values and learning that underpin our personal growth and influence our creative manifestations come from the wisdom of Walks Tall Woman, supported by the energy of Ivy, who teaches us how to work together and collaborate in relationship, honoring independence whilst understanding the true nature of healthy interdependence.

This Lunar phase was an absolute revelation to me! I have been described as fiercely independent and from an early age learned many valuable life skills that meant that I didn't have to depend on anyone and could stand on my own two feet. The teachings of Walks Tall Woman helped me to understand the nature of self-sabotage when independence becomes a defense that keeps people out, creating a complete imbalance of giving and receiving. As a consistent over-giver, I needed to significantly review the underlying reasons that caused me to give without discernment, inadvertently creating situations where I welcomed a continuous stream of the wrong kinds of people into my world.

Walks Tall Woman teaches us to stand strong and not be affected by the insecurities of others. She invites us to make a firm commitment to ourselves and to understand the difference between healthy pride, when we honor our achievements including our mistakes, as opposed to unhealthy pride, rooted in fear and the hurts of the past, fueling a need to be perfect and approved by everyone, without enquiry or discernment.

I have no doubt that the lessons of this Lunar phase will deepen every year, gently but firmly removing the patterns within, that were inadvertently feeding and reinforcing a lack of trust in others. The New Moon in Scorpio that heralds the beginning of this Lunar phase invites us to dive deep and root out those secrets within that cause us ongoing difficulty. The Full Moon in Taurus also known as Beaver Moon, Frost Moon, and Ivy Moon, highlights our insecurities, giving us opportunity to release repeating patterns and invest fully in building healthy self-esteem based on self-respect, and the integrity of firm boundaries.

RED CALCITE

Red Calcite.
Aligning with the Eleventh Moon Phase Walks Tall Woman.
Discernment, strength, and collaboration.

Red Calcite is associated with an enthusiasm and passion to live life to the full. Full of vitality it enhances and empowers a passion for life, whilst simultaneously grounding and centering, bringing protection and affirming strong boundaries, easing any lethargy or confusion of direction. It is also said to be a major ally when dealing with people who consistently step over our boundaries or have unrealistic expectations as to what and how much we should be giving them!

For myself, when I find myself trying to spin too many plates at once resulting in my going around in circles and not really attending to anything, this powerful stone will help me to put the brakes on without losing any energy, I can then get focused and apply myself to each task with passion and renewed vitality. Associated with the Root Chakra it plays a key role in supporting our capacity for conscious manifestation.

25th October - New Moon Eclipse in Scorpio

The energy of a New Moon in Scorpio naturally lends itself to wishes that embrace areas of change and personal transformation that go deep… and it's eclipse season.

The overall Lunar energy today invites us to focus our attention within, letting go of any inner beliefs that limit our potential, whilst leaning into a space of new horizons. Eclipse season is said to open portals of potential, where through meditation and journeying we can access the timeline of our soul's evolution, bringing restoration to past issues, generating creative opportunity in the present, with a vision of the future we wish to manifest.

A Scorpio New Moon naturally lends its energy to support wishes that focus on empowerment through self-mastery, transformation, letting go of power struggles, partnerships, deep Soulmate connections and our sensuality and sexuality and even though our beautiful Moon is squaring up with Pluto, the overall dynamics invite us to lean into this energetic and use this powerful space as a source of personal transformation.

In your New Moon ceremonies write down your 10 wishes and open yourself to receive the guidance that you need to highlight the next steps on your pathway of manifestation.

To engage with the New Moon energy at its most powerful, be sure to write your wishes down during the 8 hours following the exact time of the New Moon in your location.

- **25th October - Los Angeles 03.48**
- **25th October – New York 06.48**
- **25th October - London 11.48**
- **25th October – Sydney 21.48**
- **25th October – Auckland 23.48**

My Ten New Moon Wishes

1

2

3

4

5

6

7

8

9

10

My Wishes and Dreams

My Ten New Moon Intentions

1

2

3

4

5

6

7

8

9

10

My Intentions Are...

8th / 9th November - Full Moon Eclipse in Taurus

The energy of a Full Moon in Taurus brings perseverance and inspires us to push forwards, regardless of any obstacles in our path. When our actions are in pursuit of higher ideals, the energy flow will work with us bringing us staying power and stamina, however we must also be mindful not to act like a bull in a china shop pushing through without thought or regard and so a Taurus Full Moon will also highlight areas of our lives where we perhaps need to slow down and tread a little more lightly.

A Taurus Moon will also naturally focus our attention on security and stability and so the added influence of the Eclipse may well bring to light any insecurities that we need to attend to, particularly around home, family, finances, and health. And this will include the health of our self-esteem and emotional wellness as well.

If you find yourself wanting to stay at home and retreat, listen to this calling and go to ground. The influence of the great communicator Mercury creates opportunities for conversations of significant enlightenment, out in the world with others, and also within ourselves.

Each month place some rainwater or spring water in a bowl and leave it out overnight to absorb the energy of the Full Moon. Do NOT use a plastic bowl! Use glass or earthenware or any container whose fundamental ingredients come from a natural source. Collect the water afterwards and store it in a jar.

Use this Moon Water in any of your ceremonies where you need to find perseverance and staying power, or perhaps to slow something down to a manageable pace bringing slow and steady progress.

- **8th November - Los Angeles 03.01**
- **8th November – New York 06.01**
- **8th November - London 11.01**
- **8th November – Sydney 22.01**
- **9th November – Auckland 00.01**

My Full Moon Insights and Illuminations

Journaling and Notes

Journaling and Notes

The Eleventh Moon Phase

Journaling and Notes

Journaling and Notes

Journaling and Notes

Journaling and Notes

Journaling and Notes

Reflections from the Eleventh Moon Phase

The Twelfth Moon Phase of 2022

Gives Praise – Cold Moon – Long Nights Moon – Reed Moon

23rd November – 22nd December

Key Astrological Dates

- **23rd November - New Moon 01°37' Sagittarius**
- **4th December - Neptune retrograde ends**
- **8th December - Full Moon 16°01' Gemini**
- **21st December - Winter Solstice Northern Hemisphere – Summer Solstice Southern Hemisphere**
- **22nd December – Sun enters Capricorn**
- **23rd December - Chiron retrograde ends**
- **23rd December - New Moon 01°32' Capricorn**

During this Lunar month the values and learning that underpin our personal growth and influence our creative manifestations come from the teachings of Gives Praise, supported by the energy of Reed bringing us resilience and grace, even in the face of adversity or challenge.

For me, the lessons of this Lunar phase embody the essence of what manifestation is truly about. During this Moon time so many situations, some small and some very big, seemed to miraculously appear in my world, demonstrating so clearly that abundance comes to us from the inside out and is massively influenced by our perceptions, attitudes, and state of mind.

Gives Praise teaches us about the magic of congruence and authenticity. By becoming who and what we wish to see in the world and through living the essence of those values, we then attract more of the same.

During this Moon cycle I became very conscious of my thoughts and words. It is so easy to present the universe with our wishes and desires whilst simultaneously holding many negative thoughts and beliefs. Sometimes we use the phrase, 'empty words'. This doesn't mean that the words are empty of meaning, it simply means that the words are not congruent with the actions that follow. When words are empty or have a different intent to that which is being spoken, then the laws of attraction will respond to the underlying truth of the language presented. Negative thoughts magnetize and magnify difficulties whilst gratitude magnetizes and attracts abundance.

The power and magic of abundance is having the right attitude... and meaning it... and knowing it... and being it... and doing it! This is congruence, and the core recipe for success and abundance. The New Moon in Sagittarius naturally invites us to step into a space of optimism surrounding our wishes and intentions with positivity, determination, and grace. The Full Moon in Gemini also known as Cold Moon, Long Nights Moon and Reed Moon, illuminates any internal contradictions in our thinking patterns and behaviors and through this awareness, opens the doorway to resolution and congruence within. The energy of the Solstice concludes this Moon time, inviting us to pause for breath, and to anchor ourselves into an attitude of gratitude.

RAINBOW FLUORITE

Rainbow Fluorite.
Aligning with the Twelfth Moon Phase Gives Praise
The laws of attraction!

Fluorite comes in many colors and is known as a great emotional stabilizer. It puts the breaks on when our mind races and we feel ourselves spiraling into emotional overload. Bringing our chakras into alignment in a very particular way it is said to allow us to see our situation through a different lens. As such it is a major helper if we suffer from habitual thinking patterns that cloud our judgement and block us from approaching our situation in a grounded and realistic manner.

Rainbow fluorite is said to be particularly helpful in work settings where we feel easily overloaded. Simply holding this crystal for a short while will bring clarity and calm releasing any emotional toxicity that may cloud our judgement.

23rd / 24th November - New Moon in Sagittarius

The dynamics of this New Moon are just gorgeous!

The energy of the New Moon in Sagittarius naturally embraces the qualities of renewed optimism, holding hope, overcoming depression, and the finding of solutions. This energetic also naturally enhances any wishes that connect with our personal sense of freedom, the rights and freedom of others, truth, liberty, and justice. Wishes set at this time are also perfect in bringing increased motivation, with stamina and determination to see something through.

If you have struggled with procrastination, then this is a perfect New Moon to request that these thinking patterns leave you and are easily let go of, and if you are seeking spontaneity and adventure and have been searching to find your calling to align you with renewed energy, hope and inspiration, this is a perfect time to request signposts to show you what steps to take next to bring a clarity of direction easily and quickly.

The Lunar energy loosely trines with both expansive Jupiter, who is also the ruler of Sagittarius, and with the passionate energy of Lilith, who has been calling us to honor entitlement. With transformational Pluto also radiating positive energy, the astro-dynamics of this New Moon beautifully support the setting of wishes and intentions that infuse any and all of our manifestations with inspiration and renewed passion and enthusiasm.

In your New Moon ceremonies write down your 10 wishes and open yourself to receive the guidance that you need to highlight the next steps on your pathway of manifestation.

To engage with the New Moon energy at its most powerful, be sure to write your wishes down during the 8 hours following the exact time of the New Moon in your location.

- **23rd November - Los Angeles 14.57**
- **23rd November – New York 17.57**
- **23rd November - London 22.57**
- **24th November – Sydney 09.57**
- **24th November – Auckland 11.57**

My Ten New Moon Wishes

1

2

3

4

5

6

7

8

9

10

My Wishes and Dreams

My Ten New Moon Intentions

1

2

3

4

5

6

7

8

9

10

My Intentions Are...

7th / 8th December - Full Moon in Gemini

A Gemini Full Moon governs areas of our personality and development that connect to learning, reading, writing speaking, listening and all areas of communication. The Full Moon in Gemini will illuminate any aspects of our lives that can be extended, grown, and developed further to enhance better and more fluent communication, whether with ourselves or with others.

Sometimes this Moon will bring illuminations that show all aspects of a situation and whilst on occasion this can create confusion or indecision, the value of this influence is to give us full awareness so we can then make conscious decisions.

Today our beautiful Moon sits with the masculine warrior energy of Mars! This could be quite an explosive mix and passions may run high. Passionate Lilith calling for justice and equality is also sitting exactly opposite transformational Pluto in pragmatic Capricorn.

To use this energy at its best, rather than engaging in any fast and furious re-actions, take time to reflect before responding. If you find yourself experiencing heightened positive emotions then ride the waves and enjoy… however, if you find yourself experiencing heightened negative emotions then press the pause button and take a minute's silence to re-anchor yourself, and then review all aspects of your situation before moving forwards.

Each month place some rainwater or spring water in a bowl and leave it out overnight to absorb the energy of the Full Moon. Do NOT use a plastic bowl! Use glass or earthenware or any container whose fundamental ingredients come from a natural source. Collect the water afterwards and store it in a jar.

Use this Moon Water in any of your ceremonies where you need to step back and understand all sides of the story to find clarity of vision and a clear way forward.

- **7th December - Los Angeles 20.07**
- **7th December – New York 23.07**
- **8th December - London 04.07**
- **8th December – Sydney 15.07**
- **8th December – Auckland 17.07**

My Full Moon Insights and Illuminations

The Twelfth Moon Phase

Journaling and Notes

Journaling and Notes

Journaling and Notes

The Twelfth Moon Phase

Journaling and Notes

Journaling and Notes

The Twelfth Moon Phase

Journaling and Notes

Journaling and Notes

Journaling and Notes

Reflections from the Twelfth Moon Phase

The Twelfth Moon Phase

The Thirteenth Moon Phase of 2022

Becomes Her Vision – Elder Moon

23rd December – 20th January

Key Astrological Dates

- **23rd December - New Moon 01°32' Capricorn**
- **23rd December - Chiron retrograde ends**
- **29th December – Mercury retrograde begins**
- **6th January 2023 – Full Moon 16°21' Cancer**
- **12th January – Mars retrograde ends**
- **18th January 2023 – Mercury retrograde ends**
- **21st January 2023 - Moon 01°32' Aquarius**

At this Lunar time, the values and learning that underpin our personal growth and influence our creative manifestations come from the wisdom of Becomes Her Vision, supported by the energy of Elder. In Celtic Tree Lore, Elder is the embodiment of the feminine, and the holder of sacred lore, and so it is hardly surprising then that her essence is aligned with this final Moon phase of the year.

As I read the story of Becomes Her Vision, I found myself feeling very small, and yet also inspired to strive to become a bigger and better version of myself. This Moon time moved me into a space of deep personal reflection, and as I considered the gifts and qualities of each Moon of learning over the last twelve months, I came to understand that manifestation is not an end goal! It is an ongoing journey, and that who I am and who I become on the inside, will be reflected in the world that I'm creating on the outside. The New Moon in Capricorn honors this learning, and combined with the Full Moon in Cancer, forms a bridge of steady growth, nurture, and kindness, to carry us into a New Year of opportunity and possibility.

Becomes her Vision is the embodiment of all of the life lessons held and offered to us during each of the twelve Moons, combined and transformed into a knowing and a wisdom that connects us to the sacred lore's of life. In such a humble way, I came to see that whilst we are unique individuals with the empowerment of free will and personal choice, we are also an integral part of the whole. For our human lives to be lived to the fullest we will be presented with many challenges, each one an entry point into newer and higher levels of consciousness.

Our personal evolution and the way in which we choose to live radiates beyond the immediacy of our own lives, affecting all who we come into contact with and also stretching into the future, benefit ourselves and the lives of generations yet to come. When we embrace the pathway to wholeness through individual expression and yet also strive for oneness, the illusion of separateness disappears in the face of the truth and love of all prevails.

ROSE QUARTZ

Rose Quartz.
Aligning with the Thirteenth Moon Phase Becomes her Vision.
The highest vibration of love.

Rose Quartz is a stone of universal love. It is said to restore trust and to bring about peace and harmony, healing relationship wounds not only between ourselves and others but also in our relationship with ourselves. Its highest vibration of love is said to encourage unconditional love in all forms, its energy purifying and opening the heart Chakra, promoting love, self-love, friendship, deep inner healing, and feelings of peace. It is also said to dispel negativity and protect against any form of environmental pollution, including the negative energy and attitudes of other people around you, replacing it with loving vibrations.

23rd December - New Moon in Capricorn

This last New Moon of the year in Capricorn invites us to get clear. What really matters to you? What have you learned from this extraordinary year of 2022 and what do you wish to focus on and manifest in the coming year of 2023?

A Capricorn Moon is perfect for making wishes that focus on your ambitions, goals and personal desire for success and recognition. Give yourself full permission to listen to those desires that call from your heart, as well as your mind. If you are aware of any inner blocks to your success, such as self-doubt or a lack of confidence, this is the perfect time to make wishes that support the release of any form of self-sabotaging thinking patterns or behaviors.

This is a perfect Moon to focus on your future, think about your long-term goals, and take a structured approach to the potential that you wish to step into in the coming year of 2023. You may also want to request to be shown the next pragmatic and practical steps to manifest this into being.

Our beautiful New Moon today aligns with expansive Jupiter inviting us to open our eyes to the potential in every situation and use our learning to inform our desires of manifestation for the coming year, and transformational Pluto flows with illuminating Neptune, so in preparation of your New Moon wishes, observe your past, lean into the dreamtime of your future, then get present and make a constructive pragmatic list of intentions that support your New Moon wishes and desires.

In your New Moon ceremonies write down your 10 wishes and open yourself to receive the guidance that you need to highlight the next steps on your pathway of manifestation.

To engage with the New Moon energy at its most powerful, be sure to write your wishes down during the 8 hours following the exact time of the New Moon in your location.

- **23rd December - Los Angeles 02.16**
- **23rd December – New York 05.16**
- **23rd December - London 10.16**
- **23rd December – Sydney 21.16**
- **23rd December – Auckland 23.16**

My Ten New Moon Wishes

1

2

3

4

5

6

7

8

9

10

My Wishes and Dreams

My Ten New Moon Intentions

1

2

3

4

5

6

7

8

9

10

My Intentions Are...

6th / 7th January 2023 - Full Moon in Cancer

A Cancer Full Moon naturally puts us in touch with our emotions, highlighting and illuminating areas of our lives that need gentle nurture and support.

The overall dynamics of this Moon invite reflection and healing and with Mercury in retrograde this is not a time to be rushing forwards. If you experience delays or setbacks, or any of your plans go astray, trust there will be purpose in the delay and that all will become clear. Having said this, the astro-energy also invites expansion.

To use this time at its best, practice the art of allowing, go with the flow, and be sure to give yourself plenty of space for reflection and actively choose to nurture yourself and your dreams from the inside out.

Each month place some rainwater or spring water in a bowl and leave it out overnight to absorb the energy of the Full Moon. Do NOT use a plastic bowl! Use glass or earthenware or any container whose fundamental ingredients come from a natural source. Collect the water afterwards and store it in a jar.

Use this Moon Water in any of your ceremonies where you wish to solidify your trust in spirit and the universe.

- **6th January - Los Angeles 15.07**
- **6th January – New York 18.07**
- **6th January - London 23.07**
- **7th January – Sydney 10.07**
- **7th January – Auckland 12.07**

My Full Moon Insights and Illuminations

Journaling and Notes

Journaling and Notes

Journaling and Notes

Journaling and Notes

Journaling and Notes

Journaling and Notes

Journaling and Notes

Journaling and Notes

Reflections from the Thirteenth Moon Phase

The Thirteenth Moon Phase

Blessings to you for the coming year of 2023

The Art of Manifestation Oracle Cards

The Art of Manifestation Oracle Cards featured in this diary are available to buy from the A-Z store at; https://www.azemotionalhealth.store/

They are also available on Amazon.

About the Author

Jenny Florence is a best-selling Author and her professional career as an Accredited BACP, UKRC Registered Counsellor spanned over 28 years working with individuals, couples and teams.

Her books include;

7 Steps to Spiritual Empathy – Learn to Listen, Change your Life! Mindfulness meets Emotional Awareness - 7 Steps to Learn the Language of your Emotions and the I Choose Love Series which includes I Choose Love – the A-Z Guidebook for the Spiritual Warrior, the Art of Manifestation Astro-Moon Diary and Journal and the Art of Manifestation Oracle Cards.

Her books are available from Amazon or from the A-Z of Emotional Health online Store.

https://www.azemotionalhealth.store/

She first began reading Tarot cards as a teenager and has also studied astrology. She posts free weekly and bi-monthly readings on her YouTube Channel which align with the natural cycles of the Moon.

She is the founder and creator of the A-Z of Emotional Health on-line Video Library, a free Public Resource, dedicated to understanding Emotional and Mental Wellness from a holistic perspective.

For more information visit her Free on-line Library;
https://www.azemotionalhealth.com/

Or follow her on Social Media;

YouTube - http://www.youtube.com/c/AZEmotionalHealth

Facebook - https://www.facebook.com/azofemotionalhealth/

Made in the USA
Coppell, TX
18 November 2021

65963057R00139